"We all need hope and encouragement. Michael Dixon provides exactly that in this book that is autobiographical, biblical and practical. I am glad to commend it to you. Read and be blessed."
Daniel L. Akin, President, Southeastern Baptist Theological Seminary, Wake Forest, North Carolina.

"Pastor Michael's book is personal, practical, and profound because it is biblical and bathed in the hope-filled power of the Gospel. Read it, follow this well-worn and proven path, and be set free from whatever holds you in bondage."
Sam R. Williams, Ph.D.
Professor of Counseling
Southeastern Baptist Theological Seminary
Wake Forest, North Carolina

"The book you hold in your hands offers a Biblical road to recovery. Pastor Michael Dixon shows through the Gospel of Christ, the principles of scripture, and personal experience how to be free from addictions. Read it, heed it, and start living life *more abundantly*.
Dr. Herb Reavis, Jr.
Senior Pastor
North Jacksonville Baptist Church
Jacksonville, Florida

CASTING DOWN IDOLS
THROUGH THE POWER OF THE GOSPEL

PASTOR MICHAEL R. DIXON

WESTBOW°
PRESS
A DIVISION OF THOMAS NELSON
& ZONDERVAN

WestBow Press books may be ordered through booksellers or by contacting:

WestBow Press
A Division of Thomas Nelson & Zondervan
1663 Liberty Drive
Bloomington, IN 47403
www.westbowpress.com
1 (866) 928-1240

ISBN: 978-1-4908-6543-0 (sc)
ISBN: 978-1-4908-6544-7 (hc)
ISBN: 978-1-4908-6542-3 (e)

Library of Congress Control Number: 2015900204

Print information available on the last page.

WestBow Press rev. date: 1/24/2015

This book is dedicated to my precious family
who have loved, supported, and encouraged me
through every ministry endeavor in my life.

To my wife, Melissa, who is always such a treasured
example to me of what a true helpmeet is meant to be.
You have helped me overcome so much in my life.

To my three daughters Sarah, Michaela, and Hannah—I am a
blessed man as a recipient of God's grace and also to be called
your dad. You are treasures in my life and I pray that you will
always worship only at the altar of the one true God of the Bible
Who created you, loves you, and sacrificed Himself for you.

A very special thank-you to my sister in Christ, Gale Hoey.
Thank-you for the countless hours you spent editing and
guiding this manuscript to its completed state. May our Lord
use our combined efforts to help others walk in freedom.

This book is also dedicated to the memory of a very
special brother in Christ and former counselee who now
has victory forever over the bondage of idolatry.

Christopher Worth Heath
02/28/1980 – 08/20/2010

Contents

THE PROBLEM WITH IDOLS

"I can do all things through Christ who strengthens me."
Philippians 4:13

We live in an increasing liberal society with decaying morals and blatant rebellion. What was called *wrong* a few years ago is now deemed *acceptable*. Many people now want to believe that truth is relative. Some even profess that there are no absolutes. People smugly state, "What is wrong for you may not be wrong for me." This is a clear indication of a civilization that is attempting to candy-coat its sin and excuse its wrongs. The result is a people barreling off course, heading at lightning speed away from God and head on into destruction. The Psalmist, referring to those who worship idols, wrote in Psalm 16:4: *"Their sorrows shall be multiplied who hasten* after *another* god."

Idolatry is not only acceptable, it is also encouraged in today's world. It is interesting that one of the most viewed reality television shows in recent years in the United States has been *American Idol*. We have become a nation that no longer recognizes the Creator Who deserves and commands our worship. Instead of worshipping God as God, we have constructed our own false gods who offer us a bogus sense of security and well-being. These idols are not restricted to the United States of America. Idols are everywhere. They are also nothing new. There have been idols as long as there has been sin in the world.

Idols have always been a spiritual problem between man and His

Creator. We were created to worship God. The Bible declares this to be true. 1 Peter 2:9: *"But you are a chosen generation, a royal priesthood, a holy nation, His own special people, that you may proclaim the praises of Him who called you out of darkness into His marvelous light."* God declares in Isaiah 43:7: *"Everyone who is called by My name, whom I have created for My glory; I have formed him, yes, I have made him."* There is an undeniable internal urge within mankind to worship. People attempt to satisfy that urge with activities, things, or people rather than God Who created them. When this occurs, idols are constructed and erected within the heart. Those idols begin to control and steer that person's life and he now becomes an idolater and ultimately even a slave to his false god.

There are many things that can become idols. In ancient days, the Hebrews, who were living under Aaron's leadership, melted down their precious metals and formed a golden calf that they began to worship. Once Moses came down off the mountain, with the Ten Commandments in hand, he was outraged that God's people would be guilty of such flagrant idolatry. Moses, in his heated anger, threw down the two stone tablets, breaking them into pieces at the foot of the mountain. He then commanded that the golden calf be crushed into powder and burned. In an attempt to teach the people a lesson, Moses had the powder deposited into their drinking water (Exodus 32). It is astounding that even under the great leadership of Moses and Aaron, God's people were still pulled toward idolatry.

Again, as recorded in 2 Kings 18:4, God's people desired to worship the bronze serpent that Moses had built for their deliverance from a plague of snakes (Numbers 21). Time and time again we find recorded on the pages of the Holy Bible, the problem with idols—even among God's people. Idols have always been a problem. They were not a problem only a thousand years ago, but they remain a real and serious problem today.

We need to understand that God is serious concerning His people worshipping only Him. When the Israelites were about to enter into the Land of Canaan, God commanded them concerning the pagan and idolatrous people they would encounter. God's command and warning is recorded in Exodus 34:13-14: *"But you shall destroy their altars, break their sacred pillars, and cut down their wooden images (for you shall worship no other god, for the LORD, whose name is Jealous, is a jealous God)."* Deuteronomy 4:24 declares: *"For the LORD your God is a consuming fire, a jealous God."* The first of the Ten Commandments declares, *"You shall have no other gods before Me"* (Exodus 20:3). God is a jealous God.

When we begin to worship someone or something other than God, we are giving our allegiance to a false god. False gods cannot bring protection, blessing, or any good thing because they are not God. However, our enemy is a cunning expert at convincing us otherwise.

Every addiction, or spiritual idol in the heart begins with deceptive messages. The Bible clearly identifies our enemy as a *liar* and *the father of liars* (John 8:44). As the temptation is realized, a person begins to believe that a substance, a drug, or even an activity can bring him happiness. Herein is revealed the deceptive plan that leads a person into the bondage of drug addiction, alcoholism, and even into pornography and gambling addictions. We begin to tell ourselves, "This will make me feel better." "It isn't hurting anyone." "This will help me forget about my problems." In the end it is realized that none of those promises are fulfilled. Instead of happiness, there is only sadness. Instead of riches, there is abject poverty. Instead of promised peace, there is now only guilt and shame. The painful aftermath of addictive behavior has not only now consumed the addict, but has also spilled over into the lives of everyone nearby. It is usually those that we love the most who bear the brunt of pain as result of these struggles.

It is not only drug addiction that we are talking about here. Addiction to pornography usually begins with the idea that we can control others through images and use them to fulfill our own selfish desires. Too many have discovered that this activity begins to control them, instead of them controlling it. It becomes an idol in the person's life. It is an idol that demands more and is never fully satisfied. The addiction draws the addict further down into the pit of despair and self-destruction.

An idol controls a person's thoughts, time, and resources. Isn't this also true of addictions? The addict begins to discover that an increasing amount of time, money, and resources is being directed toward the worship of his false god. The bondage of addiction seeks to consume all that a person is and ever hopes to be. The end result is a trail of broken lives, destroyed reputations, serious health problems, and even death. Addiction is a serious worship problem.

What should we do with idols according to God? He tells us in Joshua 7:13: *"Get up, sanctify the people, and say, 'Sanctify yourselves for tomorrow,' because thus says the Lord God of Israel: 'There is an accursed thing in your midst, O Israel; you cannot stand before your enemies until you take away the accursed thing from among you.'"* God is commanding us to get rid of the idols! Paul, writing under the inspiration of the Holy Spirit, commands us to run from idols. Paul writes in 1 Corinthians 10:14: *"Therefore, my beloved, flee from idolatry."* Instead of running toward these idols, we should run away from them! Our hearts are naturally turned away from our God. We so easily find ourselves moving in the wrong direction.

Rebellion comes to the surface through our idolatrous affections. God is, however, very serious concerning this issue. What is the consequence if we do not flee these idols? What will happen if we continue on a rebellious path away from the worship of the one true God? The warning is clear. *"Do you not know that the unrighteous will not inherit the kingdom of God? Do not be deceived. Neither fornicators, nor idolaters, nor adulterers, nor homosexuals, nor sodomites, nor thieves, nor covetous, nor drunkards, nor revilers, nor extortioners will inherit the kingdom of God"* (1 Corinthians 6:9-10).

Idolatry is evidence of a heart that has not fully surrendered to the

Lordship of Jesus Christ. It could also be evidence of an unregenerate heart. This issue must be dealt with if you want to live the life that God desires for you. You must cast down those idols. This can be accomplished only through the power of the gospel. It is not enough to simply stop ungodly behavior; we *must* replace it with godliness. We must stop bowing down and worshipping the false gods, whatever form they may take, and begin worshipping only God. This is the purpose for which you were created. It is only in fulfilling your intended purpose that you will find real life. Are you ready to begin?

FROM THE NEEDLE TO THE BIBLE

For by grace you have been saved through faith, and that not of yourselves;
it is the gift of God, not of works, lest anyone should boast.
Ephesians 2:8-9

If you are reading this book, chances are you or someone you know, is struggling in the bondage of addiction. There is hope. The hope for freedom is offered through the power of God in the Person of Jesus. As the children of Israel were taken into bondage through slavery in Babylon, God spoke these words through the prophet Jeremiah: *"For I know the thoughts that I think toward you, says the LORD, thoughts of peace and not of evil, to give you a future and a hope"* (Jeremiah 29:11). Those are God's words to you today. God desires to give you forgiveness and a brand new start. That new beginning can begin right now. It will not be easy, but you can be set free and become a new person.

I know God can give you all that you need to be delivered. First of all, I know this is true because God promises to give us freedom and deliverance. God cannot lie (Numbers 23:19). The Psalmist declared: *"He is my loving God and my fortress, my stronghold and my deliverer, my shield, in whom I take refuge, who subdues peoples under me"* (Psalm 144:2). There are many other promises recorded in the Holy Bible which we will study together in the coming chapters. These promises are from *God!* God's Word is always true and faithful.

Secondly, I also know from personal experience that God can deliver you. It was on a cold winter night in 1987 that God reached down and pulled my soul out from the pit of alcohol and drug addiction. Since that time I have chosen to walk in deliverance and freedom in the power of the Holy Spirit Who lives within me. There have been temptations, but I have chosen to be victorious over them. Do not tell yourself that you cannot be set free. Listen my friend, God has not changed! Hebrews 13:8 declares *"Jesus Christ is the same yesterday, today, and forevermore."* He is the same God with the same power for you as He is for me. Just as He has delivered me, He can deliver you. God shows no favoritism. It is God's desire that you walk in freedom and that you begin right now.

I know we all have a story to tell. Each one who has been touched by the invisible hand of Almighty God knows the undeniable power that God offers for the believing sinner. It is my prayer that God can use a small part of my story, along with His infallible truths of scripture, to speak to your heart. I pray that you will allow Him to transform you as we listen to His voice through this study. I give God all the glory, praise, and credit for what has taken place within me. This wonderful new life that I have received through Christ is what I desire for you as well. It is not only *available* for you, but God desires for you to *make it yours.*

My life has not always been a joyful experience. I have made many mistakes and chosen foolishness over godly wisdom many times over the years. There is so much in my past that I wish I could simply erase from my memory forever. Maybe you feel that way as well. Are there hidden skeletons in your closet—things that have happened in your life that you would never desire others to know? Some of these events in my past I have kept secret for many years. Some of these are shameful and to be honest, I had never planned on ever telling this story. That is until the Holy Spirit taught me a very valuable lesson: God is so mighty and awesome that He can use even my failures and all of my past mistakes for His glory. What a mighty God we serve!

He can use not only the good things in our lives, but also those things that were meant to harm and even destroy us. Trust God with your story!

I also know that as I share what God has done, my heart is healed a bit more. We all need healing. We all yearn for freedom from our past mistakes and deliverance from the wickedness the enemy has thrown at us. Jesus promised that the Truth would bring us freedom (John 8:32). Truth is found in God. God is Truth. He is the giver of life and everything "good and perfect." James 1:17 reminds me that *"every good gift and every perfect gift is from above, and comes down from the Father of lights, with Whom there is no variation or shadow of turning."* I have found in God, through the Gospel of Christ, a good and blessed life. What a good God we serve! Many times in our church fellowship we will shout in unison, "God is good all the time! All the time God is good!"

As I look back over my life, I realize how God in His goodness, has used every event in my past to draw me unto Himself. I must confess, I am not always all that I should be, even now, but I am so much more than I have ever been before. God has brought into my heart healing from the past, strength for the present, and a blessed hope for the future. It is my prayer that you, too, experience this transformation.

We all have the same problem. It is not that some have a sickness that causes them to become addicts. Our problem is *sin* sickness. We are all sinners (Romans 3:23). Notice that my use of the word *sin* is in the singular and not the plural. Our greatest dilemma is not brought upon us because of the *sins* we commit, but rather from the inherently sinful nature that we all possess. The simple yet horrifying reality is that we are all born into a sin-cursed world and we are born with sinful hearts within. My heart was naturally turned away from God and the life that only He offers. As a result, there was much loneliness, despair and pain within me, even as a child growing up in rural North Carolina.

My father was self-employed in his own heating and air conditioning business, located right beside our home. My dad was a hard worker and usually very busy maintaining his business. If he was at home, he was usually resting, reading the newspaper, or watching the news. Many times he received phone calls after hours which took him away on service calls to repair someone's heating or air conditioning unit. He was a good man who provided well for our family.

I was twenty-four years old when my father passed away on July 14, 1985, from a series of major heart attacks. There have been countless times that I have wished I could have rolled back time and enjoyed a closer relationship with my dad. There seemed to have been a great distance between us for most of my older childhood. I know that much of this distance was created as a result of my own rebellious attitude and foolish decisions. Indeed, my sinful heart had a way of drawing out my dad's faults which were usually expressed toward me in anger and frustration.

My dad's disciplinary practices were often intensely sharp and wrathfully quick. The result of my sinful nature clashing with his anger seemed to strain our relationship even more over the years. The enemy used my distant relationship with my father to grow the sinful tendencies I already had within. I remember as a young boy, I longed for loving acceptance and affirming attention from my dad. It seemed that the only attention I was successful in gaining was from his strong arm of correction. I believe that every child longs for that approval and affirmation from their father. The problem is our sinful hearts which often only scream out in pain, not knowing what to do or how to respond properly when that desire for acceptance is not received. Again, I know that my relationship with my dad would have been so much different had I submitted to his authority.

I am not a victim, nor do I blame anyone for the choices I have made. I was an adolescent boy in pain—empty inside and struggling to find my place in this world. My heart was screaming out for someone to just love me and affirm value and worth in me.

Into my starving existence, the devil sought to destroy my life using a twisted, perverted, and drug- addicted uncle who eagerly introduced me to a self-destructive lifestyle of drugs and dangerous sexual activity. This uncle has since died as a result of his destructive lifestyle. I can recall this man sexually molesting me when I was as young as eleven or twelve years old. The abuse continued over a period of several years. It was an abuse not only inflicted upon me by my uncle, but also by at least three other men who were just acquaintances in my life, but who were willing to supply me with alcohol and drugs.

I told no one what was happening because of the shame it brought me. I also felt guilty since the drugs and alcohol were a part of my lifestyle. As a young man, I had no idea how deep the wounds would be within me for so many years to come. The secret pain that I had hidden so well would follow me long after the abuse ended. Indeed, it would intend to hound me to my grave. I am eternally grateful that God had other plans.

The strange truth is that as a young teenage boy, I seemed to be drawn toward my abusive uncle. He took interest in me. He had time for me. However, the end result was not a good one. The pain and anger in my heart grew more intense, like a raging wildfire. My life began barreling downhill as I quickly found myself in trouble at school, in trouble with the police, and at odds with my parents. My father was angry with me and I was angry with him.

By the age of sixteen, I was huffing industrial chemicals, stealing and abusing valium, smoking, and even growing and selling marijuana. I thought I hated my father. As a seventeen-year-old, I had already been arrested, taken to jail for driving under the influence, had totaled my brother's car, lost my driving privileges because of fifteen traffic violations, was involved in all sorts of crimes-*and I really did not care*. There was such an overwhelming darkness in my life, birthed deep within my heart and it was threatening to consume my very existence.

One evening, while at a friend's home, I stole half a bottle of his mother's valium. That night I ingested fifteen 10-mg valium pills, not really caring if I ever woke up again. The next thing I knew it was twenty hours later and I was facing my devastated mother and my enraged father who were now threatening to send me away to a reform school. I could not remember how I made it home or what I had done the previous day or night. I later learned that my *friends* had loaded me into the trunk of a car and then dumped me in my front yard the night before. I could have died that night and my friends seemed to be oblivious to the dangers to which we were continually exposing ourselves. My life was spiraling out of control.

I wish I could tell you that this event in my life convinced me that I needed help. It *did* unsettle me. However change would not be realized in my life until several years later. There were many times over those years of drugs and alcohol abuse that I promised myself I was going to change, turn over a new leaf, and become a better person. I remember many mornings waking up in a hangover, filled with regrets and shame, longing for my life to be different. I would try to be a better person but the results were always the same because I would very quickly slip right back into my old habits time after time. *Maybe that is where you are in your struggles? Have you failed in your past attempts to experience lasting change?*

I wanted everyone to just leave me alone. I wished my parents would get off my back. I wanted the police to just give me a break. I did not want anyone telling me what I should do or what I should not be doing. At the age of nineteen, I saw a way out from under my dad's authority—marriage. I thought this would fulfill me and give me what I needed to have joy, peace and purpose. I married a childhood sweetheart who was only fifteen years old. Her father had to sign for her to get married because she was under the legal age in the state of North Carolina. I immediately moved out of my parents' home and into the home of my bride's father. My life continued as usual with one hangover after another. Following the birth of a child, our three-year marriage ended in divorce.

At the age of twenty-two, my life hit rock bottom. My wife had left me, our marriage was over, and my life was in shambles. The hopelessness in my heart plunged me into a dark emotional place where I began using drugs in a manner I had promised myself I never would. I began using a needle to shoot up cocaine intravenously. I thank God that He gave me enough sense to realize I was headed for certain ruin and a premature death. Some of my drug buddies had already died, some died from overdoses and some were dying from the HIV/AIDS virus because of contaminated needles. I was still hurting and I was more confused and lonely than ever before.

Into my painful existence, God sent a special woman, Melissa, and in 1986 we were married. My substance abuse continued, however, and just two years into our marriage we were struggling to keep it all together. My mother has always been God's instrument in my life and God has used her in a tremendous way to bring me to where I am today. Even after all the pain I had caused my mother through my teenage years and into young adulthood, she was still there reminding me that God was waiting for my total surrender. My wife, Melissa, and I knew we needed a power beyond ourselves to heal our hearts and to save our marriage. Upon my mother's urging, we visited her church for a midweek prayer meeting. It was in that service that the Holy Spirit broke through the hardness of our hearts. Melissa and I, kneeling together at the altar in brokenness, surrendered to Christ and received a forgiveness that we had never thought possible.

For the first time in my life, there was an overwhelming presence of love and hope within my soul. A great burden was lifted and an indescribable peace was realized at last. I knew when I rose to my feet that this twenty-seven-year-old man had received new power. I had been given power to change, power to love, power to forgive, the power of God to do what I had failed so many times to accomplish. Since that night in 1988 I have never turned back. I have been drug-free since that wonderful night when God touched me and filled me with His Spirit.

What made the difference between that night and all the other times in my life that I had attempted change? This time I was no longer looking to myself for the strength I needed. My past had taught me that *my* strength was not enough. Now I was totally relying upon God and I had finally opened my heart to the eternal impact of the Gospel of Christ. I understood in my inner man that Christ had not only died *for* me but *as* me. He was buried in a tomb in my place. Then on the third day, Jesus arose from the dead victorious over death, hell, and the grave. He did all this in my place, as my substitute! This was not only accomplished for me but as me. All I needed to do was place my heart faith in Christ, who is the Gospel, and my life would never be the same.

The power of the gospel is a soul-saving, life-changing, eternally-transforming power and that power is available to you right now. God's gift can bring you peace and healing. There is victorious power available for you through Christ's death, burial, and resurrection. Jesus did not die just so your sins could be forgiven. The gospel of our Lord is also about living now. It is my sincere prayer that as you proceed through the following studies, you will have a responsive heart toward God as He does His work in your life. In your flesh you will only fail. In our resurrected Christ victory can be yours.

ASSIGNMENT 1

FROM THE NEEDLE TO THE BIBLE

Everyone has a story to tell. We have all had pain in our lives that we have had to face and overcome. I want you to write out your story below. Include those events in your life that have shaped you into the person you are today:

_____

_____

_____

_____

_____

_____

_____

_____

_____

_____

_____

_____

_____

_____

_____

_____

_____

_____

_____

FIRST THINGS FIRST

"For I am not ashamed of the gospel of Christ,
for it is the power of God to salvation for everyone who
believes, for the Jew first and also for the Greek."
Romans 1:16

Maybe you have already attempted unsuccessfully to change many times. You may be wondering, just as I was, where you should even begin this time. There must be a greater plan, a stronger power, than what you have attempted in the past. Sincerity has not been enough. Trying harder has brought only one failed attempt after another. Maybe you have even utilized rehab programs and detox facilities, only to find yourself falling right back into those relentless habits. Proverbs 14:12 reminds us, *"There is a way that seems right to a man, But its end is the way of death."* If all of man's ways and plans have failed you in your attempts to break free from addiction, take heart my friend, for there is a greater power available.

God has given to us a book which teaches us how to overcome sin in our lives and how to walk victoriously in this world. I know your heart longs for that victory. Our journey begins with this question; "Where do you stand in relationship with God?" This is where we must begin. If you are sincere about desiring lasting change in your life, there is a wonderful hope for you. This hope will not be found in your intelligence or strength, nor is it offered by the worldly experts among us. We must take first things first.

If you desire God's power to change you, you must first receive that power into your life. What does God tell us must happen in order for us to be right with Him? The Book of Romans is a great place to begin answering this very important question. God spoke through the Apostle Paul to write the Book of Romans. In fact, of the twenty-seven books found in the New Testament, God chose Paul to write at least thirteen of them. What an honor that God chose Paul to write at least half of the New Testament! Paul was a person just like you and I. Paul was a flesh-and-blood man, with sinful tendencies that pulled at him constantly. This great apostle was not created as some *superman* able to accomplish things that are unattainable for us.

You might not be aware of it, but Paul was a recovered addict as well. He really was! Here was a man who was addicted to manmade religion before he came to know Christ. Paul, previously referred to as Saul in the scripture, bowed down and worshipped the idol of religion before Christ saved him on the road to Damascus. Paul confessed that he was among the most religious as he was *"circumcised the eighth day, of the stock of Israel, of the tribe of Benjamin, a Hebrew of the Hebrews; concerning the law, a Pharisee; concerning zeal, persecuting the church; concerning the righteousness which is in the law, blameless"* (Philippians 3:5-6).

Religion had become Paul's "drug" of choice and it controlled his life. He persecuted the church as a very religious man, but he was very wrong. Following his salvation experience, Paul became a giant of the Christian faith. (Acts 9 records Paul's personal conversion experience). God could now use him not only to write much of the New Testament, but also to plant several New Testament churches in different parts of the world. It is amazing what great things God did in and through this man's life once he stopped looking to his own power and simply trusted Christ instead.

You, too, will be amazed at what God will do in your life once you surrender your all to Him. God used Paul to write the Book of Romans which contains the most complete summary of Christian doctrine found in any one book in the Holy Bible. In the Book of Romans, you will find answers to questions such as: "How can I experience true freedom in my life?" "How does a person receive forgiveness and salvation from God?" "How is this forgiveness even possible?" "Whom does God desire to save?" "What does God's salvation really mean for me in my own personal struggles?" The Holy Spirit, through Paul, teaches us the crucial answers to those soul-stirring questions. This is where we must begin. First things first—and the place we must start is with our own personal response to the Gospel of Jesus Christ.

The Book of Romans lays out for us a road that we can follow to receive forgiveness and the power leading to real and lasting change. Today, as I was awakened in the very early morning hours, I was reminded of how God's power is so available to us, and yet so often hindered. Suddenly my electric fan turned off. Our air conditioner stopped. There was an eerie silence suddenly engulfing and filling our home. We had suffered a residential loss of electrical power. I would later learn that a tree had fallen on a nearby power line and knocked out our electricity for a brief time. Although I was aware that our source of electricity was disabled, I still found myself habitually flipping on light switches and adjusting the thermostat. Of course, each time I received the same result—nothing happened!

The reason that I had failed so many times to walk away from the addictions that held my heart captive was because I was experiencing a power failure. It did not matter how many times I tried, I did not have the power to make the needed changes last. I was flipping the switches, trying to change, but each time nothing happened. Like the electricity flowing back through the power lines once the power was restored, I needed power to flow through me. This power had to come from a greater source than anything within myself. I needed a greater power. I received that power when at the age of twenty-seven,

I surrendered to Christ, giving Him my all. I began to look to Jesus for everything I needed. God instantly repaired what had hindered me from walking in victory. My sins are now forgiven and the power of His Holy Spirit has come to forever dwell within my mortal body. This became a blessed reality for me the moment I gave Christ full surrender. Oh, God is still repairing Mike Dixon, but now I have the power I need for that change to continue to be reality for me.

So I ask you, "Do you really want to be set free?" "Do you really desire to stop hurting those who love you?" "Do you want the power to be the person God desires?" This does not come through willpower or the gaining of more knowledge, or through meditation, or through man's schemes and empty promises. There are not twelve steps or ten steps that will magically deliver you. Like me, you need to take only one step towards a Savior who is more than enough to meet your need. If you want this power to walk in victory, I urge you to lay aside your doubts, stop making excuses, and open your heart to God.

Holy Spirit power is not given to everyone, but anyone can receive Him. I must make it clear that I am not talking about repeating a prayer or simply knowing in your mind information concerning who Jesus is. I am speaking of full surrender to God, Who even right now is pulling you through the power of the gospel to Himself. This is where we must take first things first. Will you take this one step toward victory?

The Bible teaches that only those who believe in Jesus as their Lord receive the Holy Spirit. 1 John 4:15 tells us: *"Whoever confesses that Jesus is the Son of God, God abides in him, and he in God."* Jesus told His disciples in John 14:17: *"the Spirit of truth, whom the world cannot receive, because it neither sees Him nor knows Him; but you know Him, for He dwells with you and will be in you."*

So, as we begin, let us deal with first things first. What does it mean to believe in Jesus and to know God? You must understand these truths. Let us ask God right now through prayer to speak to our hearts as we examine His Word.

PRAYER: *"Dear Almighty God, Creator, and Sustainer, I come before Your throne right now as a troubled man/woman. I know that I need help. My life is a mess. My heart is hurting. I am seeking answers right now. God, reveal to me through Your Word and the power of Your Holy Spirit all I need to know. I open my heart to You. Speak to me. Change me. Help me to see the Truth. In Jesus' name, Amen."*

1. **We all have the same problem, we are sinners.**

Romans 3:10-12: *"There is none righteous, no, not one; There is none who understands; There is none who seeks after God. They have all turned aside; They have together become unprofitable; There is none who does good, no, not one."*

Romans 3:23: *"for all have sinned and fall short of the glory of God... ."*

God originally created everything in perfection. Adam and Eve, the first man and woman, were created in God's image. Then Satan slithered into that perfect sinless environment bringing with him temptation. Adam and Eve disobeyed God and as a result every person born through Adam's lineage has this germ of sin flowing through his veins. Every person born, with the exception of Jesus, was born through the line of Adam. There have been several scientific DNA studies conducted over the years that offer proof that all of mankind shares a common ancestor.

We are all born with a soul, or inner man, that wants to be self-centered and self-consuming. Need an example? We have all witnessed, or even experienced, a small toddler in a department store's toy department throwing a fit because Mommy told him he could not have a certain toy. That behavior was not learned, but was instilled within that child even before birth. The Apostle Paul put it this way in Romans 7:1: *"For what I am doing, I do not understand. For what I will to do, that I do not practice; but what I hate, that I do."* Paul sounded as if he were in the midst of an agonizing mental breakdown or suffering from bipolar disorder. No! What he is saying is simply, "I find it so easy to do wrong (sin) and so difficult to do right." To do just what comes naturally for us is to sin. Our natural man is prone to lead us in the wrong direction. We all have this problem because it is common to all of mankind.

There are many people who like to think of themselves as being good people. They would never refer to themselves as sinners since they have never committed any gross crime and they try to treat others the way that they want to be treated. Romans 12:3 warns each one of us: *"not to think of himself more highly than he ought to think, but to think soberly, as God has dealt to each one a measure of faith."*

We need to see ourselves the way that God sees us. Although most of us have never robbed a bank, murdered someone, nor committed some other heinous crime, we are still not good enough. The issues are within our hearts. Allow me to ask you, "Have you ever told a lie?" "Have you ever taken something that did not belong to you?" "Have you ever harbored lust or jealousy or hatred within your heart?" The answer, of course, would be a resounding "Yes! A million times over! Yes!" We are all guilty. The Bible tells us as recorded in James 2:10: *"For whoever shall keep the whole law, and yet stumble in one point, he is guilty of all."* So, according to God, if you have committed one sin, then you are a sinner. If you have broken one of God's laws, then you are a law-breaker. There is a penalty for breaking the law. The old expression, "Don't do the crime if you can't do the time" reminds us there is a price to pay.

2. **We all have a penalty which we owe because of sin, the penalty of spiritual death.**

Romans 6:23: *"For the wages of sin is death, but the gift of God is eternal life in Christ Jesus our Lord."*

Since we are all sinners by nature, we are all facing the same penalty for our sin which is death. When Scripture refers to death in this context, it refers to much more than physical death. This refers to a *spiritual* death. Just as physical death is the separation of the soul from the physical body, spiritual death is the separation of a soul from God forever.

The Bible tells us of a place which is prepared for the devil and his demons (Matthew 25:41). This place is referred to as hades or hell. It is a place of eternal torment (Matthew 25:46). Speaking of those who do not know God, the Bible says in 2 Thessalonians 1:9: *"These shall be punished with everlasting destruction from the presence of the Lord and from the glory of His power."* Hell is a place where there is separation from God forever. This is what we all deserve because we are all sinners. We need mercy and grace and not justice. We do not want what we all deserve. We need forgiveness. God help us! God offers the solution for you.

3. **We all have someone Who has willingly paid our sin debt.**

Romans 5:8: *"But God demonstrates His own love toward us, in that while we were still sinners, Christ died for us."*

There was only one person who has ever lived who is capable of paying the sin debt that we all owe. His name is Jesus. What makes Jesus so special? Jesus was more than just a man. Jesus was God and man. Titus 2:13 teaches us that as we anticipate Christ's return to earth we are: *"looking for the blessed hope and glorious appearing of our great God and Savior Jesus Christ... ."* Upon seeing the resurrected Christ, Thomas cried out; *"My Lord and my God!"* (John 20:28). Jesus was born of a virgin (Matthew 1:18-23). Jesus lived a sinless life (1 Peter 2:22). Jesus died on the cross and was able to pay your sin debt because He had no sin (Romans 5:8).

Why would Jesus die on a cross to pay for our sin? John 3:16-17: *"For God so loved the world that He gave His only begotten Son, that whoever believes in Him should not perish but have everlasting life. For God did not send His Son into the world to condemn the world, but that the world through Him might be saved."* God loves you! God has already paid the price for your sin *but* you must willingly accept this through faith.

4. **We all have an invitation from God to be saved.**

Romans 10:9: *"... if you confess with your mouth the Lord Jesus and believe in your heart that God has raised Him from the dead, you will be saved."*

That invitation is for everyone! The Bible says in Revelation 22:17: *"And the Spirit and the bride say, "Come!" And let him who hears say, "Come!" And let him who thirsts come. Whoever desires, let him take the water of life freely."* 2 Peter 3:9: *"The Lord is not slack concerning His promise, as some count slackness, but is longsuffering toward us, not willing that any should perish but that all should come to repentance."*

Where must you begin in casting down these deceitful

idols that bind you? You must be certain your sins are washed away and that you are God's child. You must be born again and filled with the Holy Spirit to have all you need for lasting change. The word *repentance* used in 2 Peter 3:9 means *to change*. We will look more closely at this word in Chapter 5. Are you willing to change direction? Stop trying to run *from* God and turn *to* God instead. Receive His grace and mercy, His power and love, into your heart right now.

5. **Salvation through Jesus Christ brings us into a relationship of peace with God.**

Romans 5:1: *"Therefore, having been justified by faith, we have peace with God through our Lord Jesus Christ."*

Romans 8:1: *"There is therefore now no condemnation to those who are in Christ Jesus... ."*

Romans 8:38-39: *"For I am persuaded that neither death nor life, nor angels, nor principalities, nor powers, nor things present, nor things to come, nor height nor depth, nor any other created thing, shall be able to separate us from the love of God which is in Christ Jesus our Lord."*

You can be saved today if the Holy Spirit is tugging at your heart. Do you feel conviction? Is there a restlessness within your soul right now? Your sins can be forgiven and the chains can begin to fall off if you will look to Christ in simple faith believing. Go to God right now and confess to Him in prayer:

I admit that I am a sinner.
I understand that as a sinner I deserve spiritual death, separation from God forever.

I confess right now that Jesus died on the cross for me to pay for my sins. I am now asking you God to forgive me.
I am willing to turn from my wicked ways. I repent and turn to God right now. Change my heart Lord. Save me Jesus.
I ask Jesus to be my personal Lord and Savior. Take control of my life Lord.

If you just prayed a prayer accepting Jesus as your Lord and Savior, I would love to pray for you. You can send me a note at: Pastor Mike Dixon, Sandy Bottom Baptist Church, 4568 Highway 55 West, Kinston, NC 28504; email <u>pastormdixon@centurylink.net.</u>

ASSIGNMENT 2

FIRST THINGS FIRST

1. Memorize Romans 10:9-13: *"... if you confess with your mouth the Lord Jesus and believe in your heart that God has raised Him from the dead, you will be saved. For with the heart one believes unto righteousness, and with the mouth confession is made unto salvation."*

2. Describe your relationship with God:

   _____

   _____

   _____

   _____

   _____

   _____

   _____

   _____

   _____

3. Why did you describe your relationship with God the way you did?

   _____

   _____

   _____

   _____

4. Summarize this passage in your own words:

Philippians 3:4-11: "...though I also might have confidence in the flesh. If anyone else thinks he may have confidence in the flesh, I more so: circumcised the eighth day, of the stock of Israel, of the tribe of Benjamin, a Hebrew of the Hebrews; concerning the law, a Pharisee; concerning zeal, persecuting the church; concerning the righteousness which is in the law, blameless. But what things were gain to me, these I have counted loss for Christ. Yet indeed I also count all things loss for the excellence of the knowledge of Christ Jesus my Lord, for whom I have suffered the loss of all things, and count them as rubbish, that I may gain Christ and be found in Him, not having my own righteousness, which is from the law, but that which is through faith in Christ, the righteousness which is from God by faith; that I may know Him and the power of His resurrection, and the fellowship of His sufferings, being conformed to His death, if, by any means, I may attain to the resurrection from the dead."

_____

_____

_____

_____

_____

_____

_____

_____

_____

_____

_____

_____

FACING THE TRUTH: ADMITTING YOUR SIN

"Jesus said to him, 'I am the way, the truth, and the life.
No one comes to the Father except through Me."
John 14:6

"Mirror, mirror, on the wall, who is fairest of them all?" asked the wicked witch gazing into her magical mirror in the fairytale of Snow White. The witch could not bear the truth from the mirror's reply, that there was a maiden named Snow White much fairer than she. Jealousy and hatred raged within the witch's twisted heart as she pondered a plan to destroy Snow White. There are many people today who are just like that witch. They do not want to hear the truth, nor do they have any desire to face it. Yet, as they resist the truth, they become poisoned from within as a result of the lies they are embracing.

Jesus said in John 8:32: *"You shall know the Truth and the Truth shall set you free."* Since the Truth will set you free, it seems obvious what a lie will do. Lies lead us into bondage. The enemy of our souls desires to bring us into captivity. He accomplishes this by deceiving us with his lies. Just as Jesus called out His disciples to become fishers of men, Satan and his army are also fishing for men, women, and children. I envision demons sitting high above the earth with their fishing lines dropped down upon us. Their hooks are carefully concealed within baited deceptions and lies. What is their ultimate goal? They desire to steal, kill, and to destroy (John 10:10). Once we accept the deceptive messages as truth, the enemy may then reel us in and we become hooked.

Jesus warns us concerning Satan's true nature in John 8:43-44: *"Why do you not understand my speech? Because you are not able to listen to my word. You are of your father the devil, and the desires of your father you want to do. He was a murderer from the beginning, and does not stand in the truth, because there is no truth in him. When he speaks a lie, he speaks from his own resources, for he is a liar and the father of it."* One of the devil's great lies is that we can find joy and life in what he offers through the world's resources. Yet Jesus said of Himself in John 14:6: *"I am the way, the truth, and the life. No one comes to the Father except through me."* When we believe that life can be found in anything or anyone other than God, we are being deceived. Beware my friend! Do not take the bait!

Be certain that what you believe to be true is actually God's Truth. Think about this—whatever you believe to be true, whether it is actually true or not, will affect your life. If you believe today's weather is going to be bitterly cold, you will dress accordingly. If you believe it might rain you may take along an umbrella. If you are visiting a friend and they have a barking dog that you believe will bite you, will that belief not affect your behavior? What you believe to be true affects your actions.

So many people are caught up in believing things that are not true at all. How many times have you told yourself these things, maybe under your breath? "This is impossible." "This is hopeless." "There no way I can get through this problem." "Things will never change." This list of faulty messages sent from our sin-cursed brains can reverberate through the hallways of our cognitive abilities for a lifetime.

I know that these messages which echo in my mind are not true because God tells me otherwise. In Matthew 19:26 Jesus said: *"with God all things are possible."* Nothing is impossible with God. The Apostle Paul wrote under the inspiration of the Holy Spirit in

Romans 15:13: *"Now may the God of hope fill you with all joy and peace in believing, that you may abound in hope by the power of the Holy Spirit."* God offers you hope to face any challenge in life. Paul victoriously declares in Philippians 4:13: *"I can do all things through Christ who strengthens me."* It is truth that I need! Right action proceeds out of right thinking! The enemy's battlefield is within my mind. I need truth to counter his assaults. Where do I find truth that is reliable and worthy of my trust? God offers that truth in His Word. He is always faithful and always true. That is God's nature.

Do you really desire freedom? Does your heart long for the day that you can honestly say, "My addiction is in my past? I have been set free?" If this is your desire, you must change your thinking. God offers you all that is needed for this life-changing and thought-transforming experience. Over and over again we are told from scripture to renew our minds. One of my personal favorites is found in Romans 12:2: *"And do not be conformed to this world, but be transformed by the renewing of your mind, that you may prove what is that good and acceptable and perfect will of God."* Stop clinging to thoughts that are contrary to what God says and begin agreeing with His truth instead. Let's begin with the truth of who you are.

Outside of faith in Jesus you are lost and separated from God. This was discussed in the previous chapter. We are separated from God because we are all sinners (Romans 3:23). Jesus Christ can reconcile us to God as we are told in 1 Peter 3:18: *"For Christ also suffered once for sins, the just for the unjust, that He might bring us to God."* If you have not yet accepted Jesus into your life, I urge you to return to the first chapter of this book and prayerfully read "First Things First" again. You must *first* face the truth of who you are. Outside of Christ you are a lost sinner, separated from God and His truth, and headed for an eternity separated from God and His love.

My prayer for you is that you would come to saving faith in Christ. It is only in Christ that you can experience God's forgiveness and freedom. God's desire for you is not to simply help you feel better about yourself, but to bring you to conviction concerning your lost condition so that you will turn to Him in saving faith.

We hear much discussion today concerning the topic of *self-esteem*. Experts teach that we should help our children feel good about who they are. In recent years, there have even been children's games developed in which there are no longer winners or losers for fear that losing a game might taint a child's self-image. What does the Bible say about this type of thinking? Scripture warns us in Romans 12:3: *"For I say, through the grace given to me, to everyone who is among you, not to think of himself more highly than he ought to think, but to think soberly, as God has dealt to each one a measure of faith."* Rather than feeling good about ourselves, we need the truth. The truth of who we are is found by seeing ourselves through God's perspective. How does God see you? Jesus tells us, as He told his disciples: *"You are my friends if you do whatever I command you. No longer do I call you servants, for a servant does not know what his master is doing; but I have called you friends, for all things that I heard from My Father I have made known to you"* (John 15:14-15). If you are a Christian, you are a friend of God. Before you accepted Christ, scripture says you were an enemy of God (Colossians 1:21, Romans 5:10). We must be willing to face this truth in order to be saved.

Even following salvation, we continue to make mistakes and often sin even though we have been forgiven. We all fall short. Many times when I am faced with my own shortcomings and sin, I feel unworthy of God's love. The truth is that we are *all* unworthy. This is where God's grace steps in. You experience what you could never deserve, God's salvation, freedom, and blessings in your life. God loves you! Your sins are forgiven! You are of great value in His sight!

God desires for you to experience freedom from your addiction. God is for you in this endeavor. *"What then shall we say to these things? If God is for us, who can be against us? He who did not spare His own Son, but delivered Him up for us all, how shall He not with Him also freely give us all things?"* (Romans 8:31-32). Do not rely on *self* to find your esteem. Instead, look to God for your value and there you will find an incredible sense of worth. Face the truth of who you are. You are either an enemy of God or His friend. Jesus makes the difference.

Once you respond in faith to the Gospel of Christ you become a new person. 2 Corinthians 5:17 gives us this wonderful truth: *"Therefore, if anyone is in Christ, he is a new creation; old things have passed away; behold, all things have become new."* In Christ I know that I am:

- Created in His image (Genesis 1:27).
- Accepted by Christ (Romans 15:7).
- Chosen by God (Ephesians 1:4).
- Redeemed and forgiven (Ephesians 1:7).
- Made righteous by Christ (2 Corinthians 5:21).
- A friend of God (John 15:15).
- Complete, having all I need (2 Peter 1:2-4).
- Free (John 8:36).
- Indwelt by the Holy Spirit (Romans 8:9-11).
- Loved by God (Romans 8:38-39).

Scripture teaches me even more about who I am in Christ. I must renew my mind with what God says. I need to see myself in the same manner in which God sees me. This truth will set me free from low self-worth, the feeling of worthlessness, and many other forms of mental and emotional bondage that the enemy would like to use to capture me.

We must also be willing to face the truth concerning our own sinful hearts if we are going to live a victorious Christian life. The key word in our society is *tolerance*. The world would like for Christians to soften their message. People prefer to call sin by so many other names, but fail to call sin what it is—sin. Society would rather talk about sin using terms such as weaknesses, shortcomings, affairs, mistakes and even disease and sickness. That is not the way the Bible refers to sin.

Scripture calls anything against God and His Word *sin*. I must begin to see my life through the lens of scripture. This is the truth that leads to freedom. In order to break free from the sinful habits that bind us, we must first see them for what they really are—our sins. 1 John 1:9 tells us: *"If we confess our sins, He is faithful and just to forgive us our sins and to cleanse us from all unrighteousness."* I would emphasize the possessive pronoun *our*. We must take responsibility for our own sin. Stop making excuses. Stop blaming others. Face the truth and admit your own sin. Stop referring to your addictive behavior as your *weakness,* your *crutch,* your *release.* Begin to see it and to call it what it is—sin.

You must also confess the true reality of where your addiction leads you. Realize that sin always brings destruction and pain. There is no doubt that there have been many people in your life who have been hurt as a result of your sin. It is usually those who are closest to us, like our spouses, our children, and parents, who are hurt the most. Some of them may have been hurt so many times that they no longer even desire to speak to you. You may be angry about their withdrawal from your life. Maybe you have told yourself, "They don't really care about me." Wait a minute! You must remember *whose* sin has caused this distance in your relationships. It is *your* sin that has created this mess. Take responsibility for your failures.

You must likewise seek the forgiveness of those you have hurt. Go to those people and confess your wrongs to them while asking them to forgive you. James 5:16 instructs us to confess our sins to one another. This confession is much more than a simple apology. You may indeed be sorry for the pain you have caused them in the past, but asking a person to forgive goes beyond the apology. Confessing your sin and asking a person's forgiveness gives them an opportunity to make a choice. They can choose to let go of the pain and bitterness through forgiveness or they can refuse to forgive. That choice will be theirs.

Do not expect too much too soon. No doubt your loved ones may respond much like some of mine did initially after God had changed me. They may be thinking "I have heard this before. I think I'll wait and see. Mike will have to prove to me that he is now changed." It may take some time to regain the trust in those you have wounded. Trust can be destroyed in a matter of seconds. It will take much longer for it to be restored. Be patient just as God is longsuffering toward us.

Face the truth about your addiction. Begin to see it for what it really is. It does not bring you happiness. It does not help you. It does not deliver what it promises to bring into your life. I have never met an alcoholic who planned to become a drunk when he took his first drink. I have never met a drug addict who ever desired to be at a place where he could not just stop whenever he wanted to stop.

How does this gradual process begin in a person's heart and mind? It is the deception of the enemy making promises that will only be broken in the end. Messages like: "This will feel good." "This will help you cope." "This will relax you." "You can stop any time you want." "You are in control." All those whispers of the enemy eventually are revealed as lies.

Maybe at this point you are wondering if you even have an addiction. How can you tell? Consider your honest answers to these questions:

- Does the habitual activity take the forefront in your thoughts several times each day?
- Have you tried to quit in the past, only to fail?
- Have you turned down certain social opportunities simply because you were not able to engage in your habitual behavior if you had accepted the invitation?
- Has your tolerance level increased so that you need more and more?
- Do you have secret stashes?
- Have you been denying that you have an addiction?

If you answered "yes" to any of the above questions there is a degree of addiction present in your life that must be dealt with biblically before it destroys you. God offers you all you need to break free from the bondage of addiction through the power of the Gospel of Christ. The first step as a born-again, Spirit-filled Christian, is to face your problem honestly. Confess the truth that your addiction is sin and you *must* deal with it.

PRAYER: *Dear Heavenly Father, I confess that I need You in my life. You are holy. You are true. You are God. I admit that my life is not always reflective of You. Please forgive me of my sins, dear God. Help me to see my own faults through Your eyes. I must stop making excuses for my sin. I must stop blaming others for my sin. I confess that I have been guilty of worshipping idols. Please have mercy upon me, oh God. Help me to walk in Your power. I long to be set free from the idolatry and I know that You are more than able to set me free. Do a great and mighty work in my heart and in my life. My longing is to live for You. In Jesus' name, Amen.*

ASSIGNMENT 3

FACING THE TRUTH:
ADMITTING YOUR SIN

1. Check any of the thoughts that you have had concerning yourself:

    ___I am a failure. (Philippians 4:13)

    ___I have mental problems. (1 Corinthians 2:16)

    ___I am not good enough. (Ephesians 1:6)

    ___I am stupid. (Proverbs 2:6-7)

    ___No one loves me. (John 15:9)

    ___I am unworthy. (Colossians 1:14, 20)

    ___My life is out of control. (Ephesians 2:10)

    ___I am all alone in life. (Romans 8:38-39)

    ___I am afraid. (Psalm 34:4)

    ___I am unwanted. (Romans 8:16-17)

    ___I am condemned. (Romans 8:1)

    ___I am hopeless. (Romans 15:13)

    ___I am so messed up. (Hebrews 10:14)

    ___I am already defeated. (Romans 8:37)

2. Now for each one of the above items that you checked, lookup and read the scripture appearing next to it.

3. Begin writing a list of the negative consequences of your addictive behavior. This will help you see your addiction correctly.

_____

_____

_____

_____

_____

_____

4. During the next several weeks keep an ongoing journal in which you list the ways you have kept your secret addiction hidden from others. Include in this list any manner in which you have deceived others. Where there is addiction there is always a web of deceit.

_____

_____

_____

_____

_____

_____

_____

_____

5. Ask God to reveal to you how you have hurt others in your life because of your sinful behavior. Go to these individuals confessing your sin and asking them to forgive you.

BULL'S-EYE LIVING

"Therefore, whether you eat or drink, or whatever
you do, do all to the glory of God."
1 Corinthians 10:31

Why do you desire change in your life? This is the next area we must examine if you are going to be set free from the bondage that pulls at your heart. In the previous sessions, we have discussed your relationship with God and how you can receive His salvation and power. I pray that you responded in faith and that now you have assurance that your sins have been forgiven and God has come to dwell within your mortal body. You now have the power of God within you to change!

We have also discussed the need to face the truth concerning who you are and the sin in your life. You must be willing to admit and confess your sin. Call it what God calls it. It is nothing good. Sin is destructive. Get it out of your life.

Our attention turns now to the reasons you desire change in your life. Upon careful consideration of your motivation you may need to adjust your aim. What are your goals in life—what is your bull's eye? Let us judiciously examine the answer to this question together.

I have spent countless hours sitting in the counseling room listening to counselees agonizing over their struggles and the initial perception of their problems. It is usually within the first session that I ask, "What is the number one thing that you desire out of life?" Overwhelmingly most people respond, "I just want to be happy." If that is the goal in an individual's life, then that person will make decisions based upon what he or she believes will bring the greatest degree of happiness. Is personal happiness the reason you desire to break free from your addictions? Is happiness your motivating desire in life?

Others respond to my question with "I just want to be successful." This can be a very relative determination since the definition of success can vary greatly from person to person. Some people state their goals in life as, "I just want to be wealthy." Others say, "My only desire is that people respect me." Are those the worthy goals that should occupy the bull's eye in living out our lives? What is it that you desire more than anything else? Give your answer some conscientious, heart-searching consideration. There is something that motivates you to live the way that you live. What is the number one goal in your life that you long to obtain? Please write out your response here:

_____

_____

_____

_____

_____

Now examine your response. This goal has become your focal point. It stands proudly at the epicenter of your existence. Everything you do is dictated by this goal. Those who live for wealth, when faced with choices, solemnly ask themselves, "What will bring me the most riches?" All they want out of life is to be wealthy. Whatever we place in that bull's eye is what ultimately determines how we live out our lives. This desire, person, or thing becomes our god.

There are millions of people who live their lives controlled by false gods. Allow me to explain. God created us to worship. John, as God allowed him to look into Heaven, saw all creation worshipping as he wrote in Revelation 4:11: *"You are worthy, O Lord, To receive glory and honor and power; For You created all things, And by Your will they exist and were created."* The Old Testament prophet Isaiah recorded the words of God saying, *"Everyone who is called by my name, Whom I have created for My glory; I have formed him, yes, I have made him"* (Isaiah 43:7). We are created for God's glory.

The Psalmist proclaimed: *"Serve the Lord with gladness; Come before His presence with singing. Know that the Lord, He is God; It is He who has made us, and not we ourselves; We are His people and the sheep of His pasture"* (Ps. 100:2-3). We were created to serve the Lord with gladness.

The Apostle Paul clarifies our God-intended and God-given goal for life. Paul's words summarize the truth of scripture as it relates to our lives being fully devoted to God. Here is what we should be aiming for. This is what should always be at the center of our lives. This is the reason for which we live and breathe and were created. Here is our bull's eye for living. 1 Corinthians 10:31: *"Therefore, whether you eat or drink, or whatever you do, do all to the glory of God."* Paul made it abundantly clear that whether I am eating, drinking, at work, at play, dealing with others, or simply dealing with myself, I am to bring glory to God. Any other goal becomes a false god, which the Bible calls an idol.

An idol is anything or anyone other than God that takes first place in your life. Even the atheist has a god. Whatever is in the number one slot in your priorities has become your god. It is at that altar that you worship. What is most important to you? To live a life simply acquiring as much wealth as possible is indeed a very shallow and ultimately worthless pursuit. I recall an unusual bumper sticker I saw years ago on a very expensive automobile which read, "Whoever dies with the most toys wins." That reflects a very self-centered and greedy attitude which will end in disappointment. When human life comes to its conclusion, it matters not how many "toys" you possess.

The goal of personal happiness also reveals that self is seated on the throne in the sinner's heart. Most people live for what they want. They instinctively go where they desire to go. They live out their lives with the attitude, "This is my life and I will live it the way I want to live it." Note how many times "I" and "me" are used in that line of reasoning.

I am reminded of Lucifer's problem before he was cast out of heaven. Scripture teaches that Satan was originally an angel in heaven named Lucifer, which means *day star.*[1] Because of Lucifer's desire to be God, he was cast out of heaven to become the devil or Satan. The Bible reveals what was going on in Lucifer's heart during his rebellion. It is recorded in Isaiah 14:12-14, *"How you are fallen from heaven, O Lucifer, son of the morning! How you are cut down to the ground, You who weakened the nations! For you have said in your heart: 'I will ascend into heaven, I will exalt my throne above the stars of God; I will also sit on the mount of the congregation On the farthest sides of the north; I will ascend above the heights of the clouds, I will be like the Most High.'"* There are at least five times in Satan's heart talk that he uses the personal pronoun "I." Satan is not the only one who struggles with an "I" problem. Undoubtedly self is the greatest idol that mankind faces today.

Let us apply this truth to addiction recovery. Many people desire to break free because they feel they are losing their families. Maybe a spouse who has been hurt so many times is now expressing that he or she cannot go on living like this. It may have even reached a point in which you have been asked to move out of your home. Often it is at this point that many addicts begin to realize the severity of their problem for the first time. I can recall countless times waking up with a horrible and physically debilitating hangover. My head would be throbbing in pain. My throat would be dry and raw. My eyes would

---

[1] Trent C. Butler, PH.D., General Editor, *HOLMAN BIBLE DICTIONARY* (Nashville, Tennessee: HOLMAN BIBLE PUBLISHERS), p.899.

be burning while my entire body ached from the top of my head to the bottom of my feet. A drug-induced hangover is not a pleasant experience. Yet, as uncomfortable as it is, the addict continues his self-destructive pattern of living. How foolish! Yet scripture teaches us in Proverbs 26:11: *"As a dog returns to his own vomit, So a fool repeats his folly."*

However, even more painful than the hangovers was the stark and disheartening realization of the pain I was causing those for whom I cared. Seeing the pain in my wife's face and the tears falling from her dark brown eyes, I always regretted my actions as a result of one of my binges. Melissa would plead with me to stop using the drugs and to stop going to the places I would frequently go. Many times I would leave home at six in the evening headed out to the bars. It would often be the next morning after sunrise that I would return home drunk and under the influence of whatever drug I could find the night before. It was in those moments when I was confronted with my wife's pain that I yearned for change with the greatest of longing. I wanted to change for her and even made promises that I would, only to fall right back into my old patterns time after time. There were some truths I did not yet understand.

First of all, I needed to surrender to God's love for me. As considered in the first chapter, my heart was sinful, fallen and leading me away from God. I needed what only God could offer me. I needed salvation and a power greater than my own in order to change.

My second problem was that my motivation for change was all wrong. I was attempting to reform myself for the wrong reasons. Some addicts want to quit their addictions because they see the mess that their lives are in. They simply desire something better for themselves. Some want to change because they want to stop hurting those that they love. Some realize the need for change only because their addiction is destroying their financial health or maybe even their physical health. These are not necessarily evil goals in themselves, but none is the one true goal for which we were created. My bull's eye in living should be the same reason that I desire to break free from addictions. My aim in all I do must be to glorify God.

How do you discover what brings glory to God? Where can you find direction to help you live your life in such a manner that you hit that bull's eye? God has given to us His guide, the Holy Bible, to teach us what brings glory to Him. He has also given to every believer the power of the Holy Spirit as we discussed in the first session. God has given me all that I need within the Word and the power of His Spirit to live my life in a manner that brings Him honor. A powerful passage that teaches this biblical truth is found in 2 Peter 1:2-4: *"Grace and peace be multiplied to you in the knowledge of God and of Jesus our Lord, as His divine power has given to us* [ALL] *things that pertain to life and godliness, through the knowledge of Him who called us by glory and virtue, by which have been given to us exceedingly great and precious promises, that through these you may be partakers of the divine nature, having escaped the corruption that is in the world through lust."* You will notice that I have capitalized the word *ALL* in that passage. A seminary professor gave me a clear definition of that word. He said, *"All* means *all* and that is *all* that *all* means." That makes it pretty clear.

God has promised to give to me all that I need for life through "the knowledge of Him" and "His divine power" which is given to me as I became a "partaker of His divine nature." Wow! I have the knowledge of God through the Word of God. I have "His divine power" through the presence of the Holy Spirit within me. That is all I need to live my life in a way which brings God glory and praise. So, how can you hit that bull's eye? When you apply God's truth to your life in the power of God's Spirit, you will hit that bull's eye head on.

As a teenager, and later as I entered my early twenties, I just wanted everyone to leave me alone and let me live my life the way I wanted to live it. I had placed myself on the throne of my life. I thought I knew best and no one could convince me otherwise. As a result I was looking to what the world offered me as I attempted to fill a void deep within. I was searching for a joy for which my heart had always longed so intensely. I was like a thirsty man trying to satisfy his thirst by drinking mud. I was like a starving and dying man feasting on trash. Nothing I tried, quenched my thirst or satisfied my hunger. I was just like those that the prophet Jeremiah spoke of in Jeremiah 2:13: *"They have turned from the living water to their own wells."* The wells that I had turned to had all been dry and unsatisfying.

I now understand that I was attempting to fill a God-shaped hole in my soul with all these other things. God created me to worship Him, to love Him, to serve Him. As long as I was living a life in contrast to the life for which I was created, I was sinking deeper and deeper into destruction and despair. I was living my life for a purpose for which I was not created. This is foolish. A carpenter in need of a hammer would never attempt to use a screw driver to drive a nail into a board. He would pound that nail with that screwdriver, but with very little success. The carpenter needs a hammer for this task because that is the purpose for which this tool was invented. Once I accepted Christ into my life, I began to study His Word and I discovered that my heart had changed. I no longer desired to live in the manner in which I had been living. The Bible began to speak to me like never before. I began to discover on the pages of the Bible, truth that filled me up and flooded my life with great joy, peace, and purpose.

God's Word began to confront my idolatrous heart. My burning desire became nothing but to honor God with my life and to bring Him glory. I quickly understood that drug and alcohol abuse had no place in my life as a Christian. I wanted *God* to control me, and not some poisonous, mind-altering substance. Paul wrote in Ephesians 5:17-18: *"Therefore do not be unwise, but understand what the will of the Lord is. And do not be drunk with wine, in which is dissipation; but be filled with the Spirit."* God should be the One in control of your life. You are created to worship Him and Him alone. That is to be the bull's eye in your life. God warns us that to bring destruction to our bodies is to desecrate that which is holy. Paul writes in 1 Corinthians 3:16-17: *"Do you not know that you are the temple of God and that the Spirit of God dwells in you? If anyone defiles the temple of God, God will destroy him. For the temple of God is holy, which temple you are."* Idols always bring destruction.

Pay attention to Proverbs 23:29-35: *"Who has woe? Who has sorrow? Who has contentions? Who has complaints? Who has wounds without cause? Who has redness of eyes? Those who linger long at the wine. Those who go in search of mixed wine. Do not look on the wine when it is red, When it sparkles in the cup, When it swirls around smoothly; At the last it bites like a serpent, And stings like a viper. Your eyes will see strange things, And your heart will utter perverse things. Yes, you will be like one who lies down in the midst of the sea, Or like one who lies at the top of the mast,* saying: *"They have struck me,* but *I was not hurt; They have beaten me, but I did not feel it. When shall I awake, that I may seek another* drink?*"*

This passage in the Book of Proverbs is the longest warning against substance abuse recorded in this book of wisdom. We are warned that substance abuse causes emotional problems (woe and sorrow), mental problems (hallucinations), social problems (contentions and complaints), and physical problems (wounds, redness of eyes). In the end, it bites like a snake! Yet the addict is so addicted that he keeps coming back for more of the same. I am now a Christian and God lives within me. My body has become His temple. When I allow self-destructive habits to develop in my life, I am attacking what now belongs to God.

God warns His people in Isaiah 48:11: *"I will not give my glory to another."* God will not share His honor and glory with idols. God declares to mankind in Exodus 20:5: *"For I, the LORD your God,* am *a jealous God."* Life is about honoring Him. What are you aiming for?

Now that you understand more fully what God says should be your life's bull's eye, does this truth affect your number one desire in life? If so, write below how a better understanding of 1 Cor. 10:31 has changed your goals.

PRAYER: *"Dear God, my Creator, Sustainer, and Lord—Your Word has taught me that I am created for the sole purpose of honoring and glorifying You. I confess that I have failed miserably so many times in the past. Right now I come before you in prayer, committing myself to no longer live for myself or for the pleasures of this world. My heart's desire is to live for You. Help me apply Your living Word to my life in the power of Your Holy Spirit that I can live victorious over sin. I pray that my motivations for change would honor You. I invite You to change my heart, my mind, my life in any manner that you desire. I belong to You. In Jesus' name, Amen."*

ASSIGNMENT 4

CHAPTER FOUR

BULL'S-EYE LIVING

1. Memorize 1 Corinthians 10:31.

2. Write 1 Corinthians 10:31 in your own words:

   _____

   _____

   _____

   _____

   _____

3. What are some of the bull's eyes that you have aimed for in the past?

   _____

   _____

   _____

   _____

   _____

4. What are you aiming for now?

   _____

   _____

   _____

   _____

   _____

   _____

5. Based upon your answer to the previous question, why do you desire to be free from addictions and to experience lasting change?

_____

_____

_____

_____

_____

6. Read 2 Peter 1:2-4. What has God given us so that we can have ALL we need to live as God intends for us to live?

_____

_____

_____

_____

_____

7. Read Isaiah 55:2. This passage says that people spend their money for things that are not _____.

8. Read John 6:35. Complete this verse by filling in the blanks. *"And Jesus said to them, "I am the _____ of life. He who comes to Me shall never _____, and he who believes in Me shall never _____."*

9. What does it mean to honor and glorify God?

_____

_____

_____

_____

_____

CHAPTER 5

A CHANGE OF DIRECTION

"Then Peter said to them, 'Repent, and let every one of you be baptized in the name of Jesus Christ for the remission of sins; and you shall receive the gift of the Holy Spirit.'"
Acts 2:38

If your goal in life is anything other than to bring honor and glory to God, then your goal is faulty. If anything or anyone else is at the center of your life, controlling your thoughts, and dictating your actions, then you are worshipping an idol. Jesus said as recorded in Matthew 6:24: *"No one can serve two masters; for either he will hate the one and love the other, or else he will be loyal to the one and despise the other. You cannot serve God and mammon."* What is it that occupies the number one slot in your life? How do you spend your time, money and energy? Is honoring and glorifying God really your most valued goal in how you live your life?

We are commanded in 1 John 5:21: *"Little children, keep yourselves from idols. Amen."* God does not tell us these things for His benefit, or because He alone deserves our worship, but He is telling us how to live life the way He created it to be lived. Since we are all created to worship, we will worship. If the person or thing we worship is not God, then we will worship at an idolatrous altar. There must be a change of direction in your life. Instead of trying to move away from

God, you must now turn and run toward Him. How is this change of direction accomplished in our lives?

I remember when I first realized that God had called me to preach His Truth. I was only about thirteen years old, very shy and somewhat withdrawn by nature. The very thought of standing before a group of people and speaking scared me to death. My response to this call was to run as hard and as fast as I could away from it. After all, my personal aspirations did not include becoming a preacher. That was the last thing that I felt I wanted to do with my life. So I started running from God.

For the next fourteen years, I tried to find a sense of purpose and fulfillment in many different things, but to no avail. It was not until I surrendered to God at the age of twenty-seven that I discovered something I had never expected to find. God's will for my life was not a burden to bear, but instead it became one of the greatest joys in my life. Once I surrendered to God's will, I discovered that preaching was a great blessing in my life. Please note, that I did not experience this transformation until I stopped trying to run *from* God and began running *toward* Him.

I needed a change of direction in order to understand that God's wonderful plan for me was not something that I should shun, but that it was a blessing I needed to embrace. Once I turned my heart toward God, it was as though a light had been turned on in my mind. I began to understand things that I had never comprehended before. The scripture tells us in 2 Corinthians 3:16: *"Nevertheless when one turns to the Lord, the veil is taken away."* As long as your heart is turned away from God, that veil covers your mind, preventing you from understanding God's Word and will. You can change! It does not matter how deep the addiction nor how strong the grip it seems to have upon your life. God is more than able to change you.

Paul, writing to the church at Corinth, gives us these words of hope in 1 Corinthians 6:9-11: *"Do you not know that the unrighteous will not inherit the kingdom of God? Do not be deceived. Neither fornicators, nor idolaters, nor adulterers, nor homosexuals, nor sodomites, nor thieves, nor covetous, nor drunkards, nor revilers, nor extortioners will inherit the kingdom of God. And such were some of you. But you were washed, but you were sanctified, but you were justified in the name of the Lord Jesus and by the Spirit of our God.'*

Paul says that there were some Christians at Corinth who were once caught up in habitual sexual sin, idolatry, stealing, and substance abuse (describe by the word *drunkards*). Paul says that people who show forth these evil works will not inherit the Kingdom of God. What does this mean? These habitual life sins are evidence of an unconverted, unchanged heart. If you have never been changed, then you have never been saved.

Paul writes that some at Corinth were once caught up in these addictions, but not any longer. Paul is saying "You used to be described by these addictions, but not anymore." Praise God—freedom, healing, and a new life are possible in Christ!

Please hear what God is saying to us in this passage. Contrary to what many would like for us to believe today, addictions do not have to be the final word in your life. The belief that *once an alcoholic, always an alcoholic* is not what God says. It is contrary to biblical truth to believe that once you are an addict, you will always be an addict. This is a lie that continues to hold many in bondage. Hebrews 13:8 tells us that: *"Jesus Christ is the same yesterday, today, and forevermore."* God set many of the Corinthians free from all these addictions. God is able to set you free, too. A change of direction is possible in your life. You can put down the cigarettes. You can stop drinking. Illegal drugs and the abuse of prescription drugs do not have to be a part of your present nor your future. The habitual pattern of lust that holds so many addicted to pornography can be lifted. There is hope offered to you through the power of the Gospel.

This change of direction does not begin with your outward movements. In an automobile there are many things that must happen underneath the hood before that car begins to actually turn around.

Messages are sent to the various mechanical gears of the engine, transmission, and steering components through the instrument panel. Moments before that automobile begins to turn, many other things are happening first.

In like manner, before your actions change, your thinking must change first. One of my favorite verses on this subject is found in Romans 12:2: *"And do not be conformed to this world, but be transformed by the renewing of your mind, that you may prove what is that good and acceptable and perfect will of God."* We are not to simply blend in with the world, but we are to stand out from the world as God's people. This difference begins in the mind. You must first change your thinking in order to change your direction. Instead of doting on your addictive behavior, you must grow to see it through God's eyes. Determine that you will despise sin as much as you have loved it in the past.

There is a biblical word for this changing of the mind. It is the word *repentance*. Repentance is not simply being sorry about what you have done. It is possible to be sorrowful and yet not be repentant. I have spoken with many people who have been sorry they got caught, but they were not willing to change through repentance. Paul wrote in 2 Corinthians 7:10: *"For godly sorrow produces repentance leading to salvation, not to be regretted; but the sorrow of the world produces death."* The word *repentance* is translated from a Greek word that actually means "reversal."[2] A person does a one-hundred-eighty degree turn around when he or she truly repents. They reverse their direction. Instead of always moving towards the idol of addiction, and away from God, they are now moving toward God.

I have always loved the story of the Sunday School teacher standing before her first- and second-grade class. The teacher was introducing her lesson on repentance and inquired of the class, "Does

---

[2] James Strong, S.T.D., LL.D., *The Exhaustive Concordance of The Bible* (Peabody, MA: Hendrickson Publishers), #3341, p.47.

anyone know what repentance means?" One little boy in the back raised his hand. The teacher motioned for him to stand. As he stood to his feet he replied, "It's being sorry about your sin." The teacher responded that was not quite the answer she was looking for. A little girl raised her hand. Upon recognition from the teacher she stood and answered confidently, "Repentance is being sorry enough about your sin to quit." That's it! A change is needed. A reversal in direction! There is a genuine change of mind and heart. This inward change leads to the change of direction that you seek in your life right now.

David gives us insight into this matter through Psalm 51. Many scholars believe that this Psalm was written approximately one year after David's sin with Bathsheba, recorded in 2 Samuel 11. Do you remember how David, a man after God's own heart, fell into sin? The scripture in 2 Samuel 11 records this event. King David was on the rooftop of his palace one evening. As he was walking upon the rooftop he noticed on the roof next door, a woman, Bathsheba, bathing. She was beautiful to look upon and as David's eyes gazed upon her beauty, his heart was filled with lust. King David immediately sent his men to go to Bathsheba and to bring her to him. King David, knowing that she was a married woman, committed fornication with her. She soon discovered that she was carrying the king's baby. In an attempt to conceal his sin, the king began to scheme. He knew that Bathsheba's husband, Uriah, was a soldier in his army. In the next battle the king ordered Uriah to be sent to the frontline and then abandoned by his fellow soldiers. Uriah was killed and King David then took Bathsheba as his own wife. It seemed that his plan had succeeded as David thought he had escaped judgment for his sins. However, God knew exactly what he had done.

The final words in chapter 11 read: *"But the thing that David had done displeased the LORD."* Sometime later, God sent the prophet Nathan to confront King David concerning his sin. It was following this confrontation with Nathan that David's heart was broken which led to his repentance. David's repentant heart is revealed as he cried out to God in Psalm 51:1-19:

"¹Have mercy upon me, O God, According to Your loving kindness; According to the multitude of your tender mercies, Blot out my transgressions.

² Wash me thoroughly from my iniquity, And cleanse me from my sin,

³ For I acknowledge my transgressions, And my sin is always before me.

⁴ Against you, you only, have I sinned, And done this evil in your sight-- That you may be found just when you speak, And blameless when you judge.

⁵ Behold, I was brought forth in iniquity, And in sin my mother conceived me.

⁶Behold, you desire truth in the inward parts, And in the hidden part you will make me to know wisdom.

⁷ Purge me with hyssop, and I shall be clean; Wash me, and I shall be whiter than snow.

⁸ Make me hear joy and gladness, That the bones you have broken may rejoice.

⁹ Hide your face from my sins, And blot out all my iniquities.

¹⁰ Create in me a clean heart, O God, And renew a steadfast spirit within me.

¹¹ Do not cast me away from your presence, And do not take your Holy Spirit from me.

¹² Restore to me the joy of your salvation, And uphold me by your generous Spirit.

¹³ Then I will teach transgressors your ways, And sinners shall be converted to you.

¹⁴ Deliver me from the guilt of bloodshed, O God, The God of my salvation, And my tongue shall sing aloud of your righteousness.

¹⁵ O Lord, open my lips, And my mouth shall show forth your praise.

*¹⁶ For you do not desire sacrifice, or else I would give it;
You do not delight in burnt offering.
¹⁷ The sacrifices of God are a broken spirit, A broken and
a contrite heart-- These, O God, You will not despise.
¹⁸ Do good in your good pleasure to Zion; Build the
walls of Jerusalem.
¹⁹ Then you shall be pleased with the sacrifices of
righteousness, with burnt offering and whole burnt
offering; Then they shall offer bulls on your altar."*

Can you hear the brokenness in David's heart? He is crying out to God not only for forgiveness, but also for change. David shows us some very important truths concerning biblical forgiveness. Let's consider these:

- True repentance means you take ownership of your own sin. Notice David states at least six times within the first four verses that he has sinned. David takes responsibility for his own personal failures. He is not blaming others nor is he pointing his finger at a dysfunctional childhood. No more excuses. You must be willing to confess and admit that your sin is your fault.
- True repentance means you stop trying to cover up your sin and you begin dealing with it. It is found in verses 5 and 6 that David confesses his own sinful nature. He confesses that God sees in the inner and hidden parts of us. You cannot hide anything from God. It is time to get real and to be honest with God. Pour your heart out to Him. He already knows everything about you anyway.
- True repentance means you acknowledge that God is the One who can forgive your sin and heal your brokenness. In verses 7-12 David seeks God's forgiveness. He also desires that God would renew his spirit and restore to him the joy of his salvation.

- o God can also do this for you. You may feel like you will never have joy again, but God can restore your heart and spirit. Life *can* be better than it has ever been before through His power and grace.

- o My life was at a point of certain ruin. My heart was empty. Then I surrendered to God's love. My heart is now full and there is a joy within me that cannot compare to anything this world can offer. What you are seeking can be found only in God. He is sufficient to meet your need. Turn to Him with all your heart. Rely upon His Truth and His power to change your heart and your life.

- True repentance brings a genuine concern for others. I know that this is true because of what God has done in my heart and in my life. I now have a special desire to help others who are now where I once was. That *can* be you. David said in verse 13 that he wanted to *"teach transgressors"* God's ways. David desired to see sinners be converted. Once you respond to God's offer of salvation in Christ and repent of your sins, your heart is motivated to help others experience what you now have. Oh, that the entire world would know the joy and the peace that Christ brings to a heart surrendered to Him! I am so thankful for the change in my life.

True Biblical repentance invites the change into your life that brings the joy and the hope you seek. Rufus H. McDaniel describes this so well in the words of his famous hymn written in 1924, "Since Jesus Came Into My Heart."

What a wonderful change in my life has been wrought
    Since Jesus came into my heart!
I have light in my soul for which long I had sought,
    Since Jesus came into my heart!

Refrain
Since Jesus came into my heart,
Since Jesus came into my heart,
Floods of joy o'er my soul
Like the sea billows roll,
Since Jesus came into my heart.

I have ceased from my wandering and going astray,
    Since Jesus came into my heart!
And my sins, which were many, are all washed away,
    Since Jesus came into my heart!

Refrain

I'm possessed of a hope that is steadfast and sure,
    Since Jesus came into my heart!
And no dark clouds of doubt now my pathway obscure,
    Since Jesus came into my heart!

Refrain

There's a light in the valley of death now for me,
    Since Jesus came into my heart!
And the gates of the City beyond I can see,
    Since Jesus came into my heart![3]

---

[3] Rufus H. McDonald, *Since Jesus Came into My Heart*, The Baptist Hymnal, (Nashville, Tennessee: Convention Press, 1991), p. 441.

PRAYER: *"Our Father, Who art in Heaven, I praise You for Your goodness extended toward me. I praise You for the change that has begun within me since Jesus has come into my heart. You have redirected my path and turned my life around. It is my desire today to walk in biblical repentance for all my days. I never want to turn from You again. You, and You alone, have all that I need for life. I turn to You with my dreams, my desires, my plans, and with my all. I love You, Lord. In Jesus' name, Amen."*

ASSIGNMENT 5

A CHANGE OF DIRECTION

1. What does the term "repentance" mean?

   _____

   _____

   _____

   _____

2. In Luke 13:5, Jesus told the people that if they did not repent they
   would _____?

3. Who was to blame for King David's sin? Was it Bathsheba?

   _____

   _____

4. Who is to blame for your sin?

   _____

   _____

5. According to Romans 2:4, God's kindness should lead you to what?

   _____

   _____

   _____

   _____

6. Describe some ways that you have tried to change in the past but failed:

_____

_____

_____

_____

_____

7. Read Psalm 51. How does David's prayer in Psalm 51 relate to you? Are there certain areas of this Psalm that you have experienced? If so, what?

_____

_____

_____

_____

8. Read Acts 5:31. Is repentance something that you do or is it something that you receive?

_____

_____

_____

_____

9. According to 2 Peter 2:9 who is it that God desires to come to repentance?

_____

_____

_____

_____

ADDICTIONS: DEAD AND BURIED

"Knowing this, that our old man was crucified with Him, that the body of sin might be done away with, that we should no longer be slaves of sin."
1 Corinthians 10:31

I trust that his study has been a great blessing to you thus far. We have talked about how we all need a greater power for change than what we find within ourselves. God offers the power you seek and need. We have also discussed how we must face the truth. Indeed, Jesus Himself said in John 8:32 that we would know the truth and the Truth would set us free. God offers truth. When we begin to see ourselves the way that God sees us, we are a huge step closer to freedom. How does God see you? Are you one of His children, born again by grace through faith, or are you lost outside of Christ.

It is also the truth concerning our sinful habits that we must see in reality. Every addiction is intertwined with lies from the enemy. We have all heard these lies whispered to our hearts; "No one will ever know." "No one will find out." "It's your life." "This is not hurting anyone." "Go ahead—it will be fun." There is of course, the familiar lie which leads into addiction, "You can stop whenever you want." Then comes the day you realize that quitting seems impossible. The addiction seems to have taken control of your mind, your behavior, and your life. Facing the truth concerning your addiction requires that you identify all these lies for what they really are.

We must also begin to see God truthfully. Your perception of God makes a big difference in how you live and what you believe. Our source for knowing God is the Word of God. God reveals Himself through the pages of scripture. The Bible reveals our God Who is all-powerful, and at the same time Who is all- loving; our God Who is a perfect, righteous judge, yet He continually extends His grace; our God Who needs nothing or no one, yet He yearns so greatly to have you near Him that He became like you, a human, and walked where you walk. Oh, yes, my friend God did even more than that. God died for you and in your place to pay a debt you could not pay.

What is the greatest sacrifice that a person can make? Jesus tells us in John 15:13: *"Greater love has no one than this, than to lay down one's life for his friends."* For a person to willingly sacrifice his life to protect another life is the ultimate sacrifice and the greatest expression of love. We often refer to such a person as a *hero.* Yet the hero of all heroes is our Lord Jesus Christ. He did not only lay down His life for us, but He was perfect in every way, innocent on every level, and blameless of any wrong. There is no other person who has ever lived that can claim this. What would motivate the perfect Son of God to willingly lay down His life for you? *"For God so loved the world that He gave His only begotten Son, that whoever believes in Him should not perish but have everlasting life"* (John 3:16). Indeed, it was God's love that brought this sacrificial death for you. Jesus died in your place!

Why was such a price for sin demanded? God is Holy and Righteous and any rebellion, any wrong, anything that is not holy or righteous must be dealt with. There is a price for sin that must be paid to satisfy the righteousness of Holy God. That sacrifice is Jesus. *"For He made Him who knew no sin to be sin for us, that we might become the righteousness of God in Him"* (2 Corinthians 5:21).

Those who have been exposed to the gospel and believed, would agree that Jesus died for our sins. But that is not all that His death brings to us, although that is a wonderful truth. Jesus not only died for you—He also died *as* you. Jesus died not to simply pay a debt that you owed and that you could not pay, but He died in your place! He died not only to offer you life in the *sweet by and by,* but He died to give you life in *the not-so-sweet here now and now."* The power of Christ's crucifixion changes us now. A.W. Tozer writes, "The cross will cut into our lives where it hurts worst, sparing neither us nor our carefully cultivated reputations. It will defeat us and bring our selfish lives to an end."[4] There is a tremendous blessing in the present through Christ's death in the past.

This is where freedom from past behaviors and addictions can be realized once we understand this truth. There is great power in Christ's death on the cross to free you from bondage. We will examine this eternal truth more closely in a moment. First, let us turn our attention to the biblical record of Christ's death upon the cross. According to Matthew's gospel, once Jesus was arrested and brought before a mock trial He stood before those in authority. This is recorded in Matthew 27:11-38:

> *"[11] Now Jesus stood before the governor. And the governor asked Him, saying, 'Are You the King of the Jews?' So Jesus said to him, 'It is as you say.'*
> *[12] And while He was being accused by the chief priests and elders, He answered nothing.*
> *[13] Then Pilate said to Him, 'Do You not hear how many things they testify against You?'*
> *[14] But He answered him not one word, so that the governor marveled greatly.*
> *[15] Now at the feast the governor was accustomed to releasing to the multitude one prisoner whom they wished.*

---

[4] A.W. Tozer, *The Radical Cross,* (Camp Hill, Pennsylvania: WingSpread Publishers, 2009), p.5.

¹⁶ And at that time they had a notorious prisoner called Barabbas.

¹⁷ Therefore, when they had gathered together, Pilate said to them, 'Whom do you want me to release to you? Barabbas, or Jesus who is called Christ?'

¹⁸ For he knew that they had handed Him over because of envy.

¹⁹ While he was sitting on the judgment seat, his wife sent to him, saying, 'Have nothing to do with that just Man, for I have suffered many things today in a dream because of Him.'

²⁰ But the chief priests and elders persuaded the multitudes that they should ask for Barabbas and destroy Jesus.

²¹ The governor answered and said to them, 'Which of the two do you want me to release to you?' They said, 'Barabbas!'

²² Pilate said to them, 'What then shall I do with Jesus who is called Christ?' They all said to him, 'Let Him be crucified!'

²³ Then the governor said, 'Why, what evil has He done?' But they cried out all the more, saying, 'Let Him be crucified!'

²⁴ When Pilate saw that he could not prevail at all, but rather that a tumult was rising, he took water and washed his hands before the multitude, saying, 'I am innocent of the blood of this just Person. You see to it.'

²⁵ And all the people answered and said, 'His blood be on us and on our children.'

²⁶ Then he released Barabbas to them; and when he had scourged Jesus, he delivered Him to be crucified.

27 Then the soldiers of the governor took Jesus into the Praetorium and gathered the whole garrison around Him.

28 And they stripped Him and put a scarlet robe on Him.

29 When they had twisted a crown of thorns, they put it on His head, and a reed in His right hand. And they bowed the knee before Him and mocked Him, saying, 'Hail, King of the Jews!'

30 Then they spat on Him, and took the reed and struck Him on the head.

31 And when they had mocked Him, they took the robe off Him, put His own clothes on Him, and led Him away to be crucified.

32 Now as they came out, they found a man of Cyrene, Simon by name. Him they compelled to bear His cross.

33 And when they had come to a place called Golgotha, that is to say, Place of a Skull,

34 they gave Him sour wine mingled with gall to drink. But when He had tasted it, He would not drink.

35 Then they crucified Him, and divided His garments, casting lots, that it might be fulfilled which was spoken by the prophet: 'They divided My garments among them, And for My clothing they cast lots.'

36 Sitting down, they kept watch over Him there.

37 And they put up over His head the accusation written against Him: THIS IS JESUS THE KING OF THE JEWS.

38 Then two robbers were crucified with Him, one on the right and another on the left.

39 And those who passed by blasphemed Him, wagging their heads

⁴⁰ and saying, 'You who destroy the temple and build it in three days, save Yourself! If You are the Son of God, come down from the cross.'
⁴¹ Likewise the chief priests also, mocking with the scribes and elders, said,
⁴² 'He saved others; Himself He cannot save. If He is the King of Israel, let Him now come down from the cross, and we will believe Him.
⁴³ He trusted in God; let Him deliver Him now if He will have Him; for He said, 'I am the Son of God.'
⁴⁴ Even the robbers who were crucified with Him reviled Him with the same thing."

There were many different reactions surrounding the death of Christ on the cross. These various reactions proceed from a faulty understanding of Who Jesus was and what His death really meant. The people mentioned in the Bible surrounding the death of Christ on the cross did not comprehend what was actually taking place right there before their eyes.

First, notice the soldiers who gathered around the cross that day to execute Jesus. Their attitude was one of callous indifference. These professional executioners hurriedly slammed Jesus down upon those timbers, driving the spikes in His wrists and into His feet, lifting Him up, suspended between heaven and earth. Once their job was completed, these hardened men sat down at the foot of the cross. It was there that they played a game while Jesus hung there in agony, dying in our place.

How could these men be so complacent by what was taking place before them? There, hanging next to them was a man who had been beaten almost to the point of death. These soldiers witnessed the back of Jesus ripped open by the cruel Roman lash. They saw the blood slowly fill His eyes. They heard His agonizing groans from the cross as He hung there in intense pain and suffering. What a cold, heartless attitude they demonstrated!

Yet, there are many people today who fail to recognize that Jesus was dying on that cross in their place. They would rather play the games offered by this sin-cursed world than to look in faith to the greatest sacrifice ever offered.

What was it about these soldiers that caused them to be so blind to what was happening in the death of Jesus? Their hearts had become so hardened and calloused that they were no longer convicted or even bothered by what was taking place. I would imagine that the first time they had to execute a man, it bothered them tremendously. I am sure they lost much sleep over those first few executions. Maybe they even experienced nightmares in which they heard the cries of prisoners dying in their presence. Now as they came to Jesus, they had grown so accustomed to executing men that it did not seem to bother them in the least.

This is the nature of sin and addiction. The first few times you engage in the activity, your conscience is bothered and guilt-ridden. Once you continue on this idolatrous path, you fail to realize just what is happening to you as you sink deeper and deeper into a state of hardness and carelessness. I urge you to receive the death of Jesus for you, with all seriousness and careful consideration. Stop playing the games the world offers you while Jesus is extending His forgiveness. Do not have a careless attitude as we consider Calvary's cross. Do not be complacent and indifferent toward this truth.

I also see in the biblical record of Jesus' crucifixion, the attitude of indecision. Jesus appeared before the Roman Governor Pilate. Pilate could find no fault in Jesus. Pilate's wife even warned him, *"Have nothing to do with this just man"* (Matthew 17:19). I am telling you, my friend, it is impossible for anyone to have *nothing* to do with Jesus. It is true that you have only two choices concerning Jesus and indecision is not one of them. You will either receive Jesus as your

Lord and Savior or you will reject Him. It is not possible to remain neutral concerning Christ.

Pilate was a public politician who wanted to please the people and left the fate of Christ to popular opinion. When the people shouted, "Crucify Him!" Pilate washed his hands and said, "I am innocent of the blood of this just person." It was at that moment Pilate, being under conviction—his heart stirred and his conscience bothered—that he should have accepted Jesus for Who He was. Instead, Pilate felt He could just sit on the fence and not make a decision either way. In not accepting Jesus, Pilate rejected Jesus.

I also see the attitude of unbelief present before the cross of Christ. Did you notice what the people said as they passed by the cross that day? It is recorded in Matthew 27:40: *"[IF] you are the Son of God come down from the cross."* This is the attitude of unbelief. The people failed to see Who Jesus was and they refused to believe in what He had come to accomplish. Jesus, dying there on the cross, was being much more than a good example for us. Jesus did not die on that cross only to illustrate for us how we should deal with our enemies when He prayed, "Father forgive them." Jesus was not just giving us a clear model to follow and to encourage us to stand for our convictions no matter what. No! Please do not miss what Jesus' death means for you! Do not read this with carelessness in your heart. Do not skim over these words thinking you do not have to make a decision concerning the death of Jesus. Look to that cross where Jesus died and believe today that He died there not only to pay your sin debt, but he also died there in your place!

The Apostle John, writing 1 John 2:2, declares to us this great truth: *"And He Himself is the propitiation for our sins, and not for ourselves only but also for the whole world."* Once again, in 1 John 4:10 he speaks of God's love: *"In this is love, not that we loved God, but that He loved us and sent His Son to be the propitiation for our sins."* There is a rich word that John uses in both of those verses that may seem foreign to you. It is the word *propitiation*. The English word *propitiation* in both of these verses is translated from a Greek word meaning "becoming our substitute." This is where true freedom from addiction can be realized. Jesus not only died to pay for my sins, but He also died as me, in my place, as *the propitiation* and as my substitute.

This means that as I look in faith to Christ, my past addictions and past behaviors, and everything that was part of my old person has died. Galatians 2:20: *"I have been crucified with Christ; it is no longer I who live, but Christ lives in me; and the life which I now live in the flesh, I live by faith in the Son of God, who loved me and gave Himself for me."*

I have served as a pastor since 1991. During these years I have stood by the bedsides of individuals as they have breathed their last breathe and slipped off into eternity. I have stood in the midst of grieving families in funeral home chapels where a casket stood with lid open. One thing I know is true of those who have died, they are lifeless. I see no movements, hear no sounds, nor recognize any signs of activity from that person who has died. Since Christ died as my substitute on the cross, I can claim the promise that my old man is dead. I am free from the life that I once lived. Paul wrote in Romans 6:6-7: *"knowing this, that our old man was crucified with Him, that the body of sin might be done away with, that we should no longer be slaves of sin. For he who has died has been freed from sin."* The old man is dead!

You may ask, "If my old man is dead, then why am I still tempted to live in the deadness of the past?" The influence of the old man is still present within me, but it cannot *make* me do anything. That person I used to be, no longer has any power over my life when I accept Christ's death in my place. The person I once was is not who I am any longer.

So why do so many born-again believers still allow the chains of their past to bind them? They are not recognizing the full impact of Christ's death in their place. 2 Corinthians 5:21 tells us: *"For He made Him who knew no sin to be sin for us, that we might become the righteousness of God in Him."* Jesus became sin for you! Your lust, your sinful habits, your greed, your addictions were all nailed to the cross. Colossians 3:5: *"Therefore put to death your members which are on the earth: fornication, uncleanness, passion, evil desire, and covetousness, which is idolatry."* All those sinful habits and ways of living have died and were buried in a tomb. They have no more power over your life in Christ today, *unless* you allow them to.

Following the death of Jesus on the cross, two of Jesus' followers came and took possession of His body, making certain there was a proper burial. The dead body of Jesus was placed in a grave. This is where your past needs to be laid to rest. This should be a time of beginning again in your life. You are now a new creature in Christ Jesus and old things have passed away. It is time to stand on the truth that Jesus died in your place and was buried in your place. Do not allow the influence of the old person you once were, to begin taking control of your life now.

This also means that you must put to rest any bitterness or unforgiveness that is within your heart. We have all been hurt by others. We have all been sinned against. Sin always brings with it pain and destruction. As a born-again believer in Jesus Christ, you no longer have to live in the pain from your past. That pain has been put to death.

I will never forget Saturday, August 1, 2009 as I stood in a field along with a few family members. We had gathered on this day beneath a small tree to lay to rest the cremated remains of my uncle. This was the man who had the greatest ungodly influence upon my life. This was the person who introduced me to drugs, alcohol, and sexual immorality. This was the uncle that had sexually molested me over a period of years when I was only a young boy. My family had invited me to pray at this small memorial service. I sought God's grace to help me as I sought to minister to those present that day. I had told no one of my uncle's abuse toward me with the exception of my precious wife who stood by my side. I bowed my head and prayed, asking God to help each one of us to forgive this man for any hurt that he had caused us or pain he had inflicted upon our lives. That was a moment of tremendous release for me. I believe that I had forgiven him long before his funeral, but I had not laid the pain to rest until that day as we placed his ashes in the earth. As I stood there gazing at that spot of freshly turned soil, where this man's human remains now lay covered under the dirt, I realized the power of God's healing grace for the first time in my life.

For so many years I had felt that I was so unworthy of anything good in my life. The sin which I had experienced in my childhood had made me feel as though I alone was the problem. I now understand that all these feelings, the guilt, and the shame were part of the enemy's plot to destroy me and to thwart God's victorious purpose for my life in ministry.

Even today, the enemy of our souls fights against our witness in every deviant manner in which he can. I know today that God's grace not only saves a hell-deserving sinner, but God's grace is so amazing that it also heals the sinful heart. I remain a sinner, yet saved by grace, still undeserving of anything good or godly. Oh, but His grace rescues me, restores me, sustains me, and keeps me! His grace heals the wounded heart.

What does the death of Christ mean for you? He died *for* you, but He also died *as* you. You do not have to remain the person you have always been. That old person who was addicted to drugs, alcohol, greed, lust, or whatever has been your idol has been laid to rest. Let go of the bitterness in your heart. Look to God Who loves you and offers you healing through His Spirit and through His Word.

Would you look to the cross of Christ and claim God's truth? You can move beyond your past. Philippians 3:13: *"Brethren, I do not count myself to have apprehended; but one thing I do, forgetting those things which are behind and reaching forward to those things which are ahead."* There is a new life and a new destiny waiting for you in Christ Jesus.

PRAYER: *"Thank-you, God, for dying on the cross for me and as me. Thank You for loving me so much that You became my substitute as You endured the wrath of God against my sin. My heart is burdened that such a price had to be paid. However, my heart rejoices that such a price was paid for me. I am eternally grateful. My desire is to bury my sinful past in the sands of yesterday. They are not who I am today. The old man has died. Thank You, Lord, for You have placed my past under the blood and I am now forgiven. Create in me a new heart, a clean heart. I am not the person that I once was. I give You praise for the change that has begun in me. In Jesus' name, Amen."*

ASSIGNMENT 6

ADDICTIONS: DEAD AND BURIED

1. As you think about Jesus dying on the cross what does that mean in overcoming your addictions?

_____

_____

_____

_____

_____

2. In reference to the thief dying there beside Jesus the Bible says as recorded in Luke 23:40-43: *"But the other, answering, rebuked him, saying, 'Do you not even fear God, seeing you are under the same condemnation? And we indeed justly, for we receive the due reward of our deeds; but this Man has done nothing wrong.' Then he said to Jesus, 'Lord, remember me when You come into Your kingdom.' And Jesus said to him, 'Assuredly, I say to you, today you will be with Me in Paradise.'"* There was another attitude toward the death of Jesus in this passage which is necessary for salvation. It was not one of carelessness, indecision or unbelief. Can you identify what this positive attitude was?

_____

_____

_____

_____

_____

3. Thinking back on the old you, the person you were before Christ, what are some habits, thought processes, attitudes, or actions you need to lay to rest?

_____

_____

_____

_____

_____

_____

_____

4. Everyone is a sinner (Romans 3:23) and we all grew up in a sinful world. As a result, we are all hurt because of sin—our own and the sins of those around us. Is there anyone from your past that you need to forgive? Identify any pain, bitterness or unforgiveness that is present within your heart. Write out a brief description of the manner in which you were sinned against.

_____

_____

_____

_____

_____

_____

_____

5. Go to God in prayer, seeking His forgiveness for your sins. And ask God to help you to forgive, just as He has forgiven you. Choose right now to forgive anyone who has sinned against you in the past. If possible, go to that person and tell him you forgive them. Now mark a big X across your answer to number 4 above. You have forgiven this offense and the offender. Let it go. Put it to rest.

6. Memorize Colossians 3:12-13: *"Therefore, as the elect of God, holy and beloved, put on tender mercies, kindness, humility, meekness, longsuffering; bearing with one another, and forgiving one another, if anyone has a complaint against another; even as Christ forgave you, so you also must do."*

7. Who have your hurt in the past? Who have you sinned against? List their names below:

_____

_____

_____

_____

_____

8. Go to those listed above. Admit to them that you have Sinned against them. Ask them to forgive you.

ARISE TO WALK IN NEWNESS OF LIFE

*"What shall we say then? Shall we continue in sin that grace
may abound? Certainly not! How shall we who died to sin live
any longer in it? Or do you not know that as many of us as
were baptized into Christ Jesus were baptized into His death?
Therefore we were buried with Him through baptism into death,
that just as Christ was raised from the dead by the glory of the
Father, even so we also should walk in newness of life."*
Romans 6:1-4

Thank God for His gospel! Praise Him for making a way for us to
begin again! Our God is God of another chance. Long ago, I used
to preach, "God is the God of second chances." Over the years that
sermon has evolved into "God is the God of *another* chance."

He offers that new beginning to you, a chance to begin again. The
power of the gospel does not apply simply to life beyond the grave,
but it also is relevant to life this side of heaven. I love the promise
that Jesus made as recorded in John 10:10: *"The thief does not come
except to steal, and to kill, and to destroy. I have come that they may
have life, and that they may have it more abundantly."* I have shared
that verse countless times in the counseling room with men who were
struggling and with couples in a difficult place in their marriage. I
would ask, "What do you think that word *abundant* means?" It is

translated from the Greek word *perissos* which means "exceedingly, very highly, beyond measure, more, superfluous."[5]

Jesus does not offer you just enough to get by, but He offers you more than enough. Jesus is not referring simply to *quantity* of life, life forever, but He also refers to the *quality* of life He offers. This life is not limited to the future. It is graciously extended to you in the present. The words of Jesus as recorded in Revelation 21:5 ring true: *"Behold I make all things new."* Jesus offers life to you right where you are! It is a new beginning He offers right now. Wow!

In our previous chapter we examined the truth of propitiation, meaning that Jesus died in our place, as our substitute. However, He did not remain in that cold, dead, lifeless tomb. Jesus is not in the grave today. He lives! He lives! It was on the third day, according to the scripture, that Jesus came forth victorious over death, hell, and the grave. In the same manner in which He died in our place, as us, He also arose from the dead for us and as our substitute. His resurrection offers new life for me right where I am.

Listen to Paul's words given to him by the Holy Spirit: *"Now if we died with Christ, we believe that we shall also live with Him, knowing that Christ, having been raised from the dead, dies no more. Death no longer has dominion over Him. For the death that He died, He died to sin once for all; but the life that He lives, He lives to God. Likewise you also, reckon yourselves to be dead indeed to sin, but alive to God in Christ Jesus our Lord"* (Romans 6:8-11).

Pay close attention to the last sentence: *"Likewise you also, reckon yourselves to be dead indeed to sin, but alive to God in Christ Jesus our Lord."* Paul is not speaking in southern lingo when he wrote "reckon yourselves." Paul is saying that we should conclude, or count as truth, not only that we are dead in Christ, but also alive in Him.

This all occurs through the miraculous power of the Gospel of

---

[5] James Strong, S.T.D., LL.D., *The Exhaustive Concordance of The Bible* (Peabody, MA: Hendrickson Publishers), #4053, p.57.

Christ. Just to remind us of the context in which this new life can take place, Paul writes: *"For by grace you have been saved through faith, and that not of yourselves; it is the gift of God"* (Ephesians 2:8).

Grace is God giving you what you do not deserve and cannot earn. No one deserves to be forgiven. Many years ago, I heard someone define *grace* using an acrostic:

God's
Redemption
At
Christ's
Expense.

I recently asked a group of inmates doing this study, "What do you desire—justice or grace?" The overwhelming answer was "both!"

Oh my friend, we do not want justice. If we received what we deserved, hell would be our eternal home. The story is told of a woman who was leaving the beauty parlor after having her hair done. "I hope I did you justice," the hairdresser commented as the woman opened the door to exit. The woman immediately turned and responded, "Justice? I don't want justice. I want grace!" If we received what we deserved (justice) we would all be in trouble. We are reminded in Romans 6:23: *"The wages of sin is death."* God's grace is the means whereby we receive salvation. It is also only by God's grace that we can live this abundant life that Christ said He had come to offer. Let us examine more closely what the resurrection life of Christ really means for us in overcoming addictions.

When Christ arose from the dead, according to the scripture, He arose in your place. The old you, before you came to know Jesus—the old you that was bound to drugs, alcohol, and all types of immorality—is now put to death. You are not the person that you once were. (I am also thankful that I am not what I am going to be either. God is continually conforming me into the image of

Jesus through a process called sanctification. I am currently being sanctified or transformed into Christ's image).

Jesus used the term *born again* in His conversation with Nicodemus as recorded in John 3. Nicodemus was asking Jesus questions pertaining to the new life that Jesus offered. Our Lord informed this Jewish leader that he needed to be born again spiritually, not physically. We are physically born into this world, but that birth does not make us children of God. We all have the sin problem that all humanity shares. Jesus told Nicodemus, *"Most assuredly I say to you, unless one is born again, he cannot see the Kingdom of God"* (John 3:3). The expression is true; "If you have been born only once you will die twice. If you have been born twice you will only die once."

Jesus continued in His conversation with Nicodemus and said, *"Most assuredly, I say to you, unless one is born of water* [physical birth] *and the Spirit* [spiritual birth], *he cannot enter the Kingdom of heaven"* (John 3:5). We have all been born physically, but we need to also be born of the Spirit. This is in reference to the Holy Spirit of God. The same Spirit Who embodied Jesus, is the same Spirit Who embodies you now as a believer. You have a power you did not have before. You now have resurrection power to walk in newness of life. You were resurrected the moment you trusted in Christ.

This is wonderfully good news for us as we strive to overcome temptation. We can be victorious! How do I know this is true? I see this truth revealed in the empty tomb of Jesus. It is an awesome power that can raise a dead man. In fact, it is death which is the final enemy mentioned in 1 Corinthians 15. As born-again believers, that same Spirit, with that same power, lives within us! Jesus promised His followers just before he left this earth to return to Heaven: *"But you shall receive power when the Holy Spirit has come upon you; and you shall be witnesses to Me in Jerusalem, and in all Judea and Samaria, and to the end of the earth"* (Acts 1:7-8). The Apostle Paul, writing to the church at Corinth states in 1 Corinthians 3:16-17: *"Do you not know that you are the temple of God and that the Spirit of God dwells in you?"*

Think about this magnificent truth a moment. Ponder the implications for you, my friend. The Holy Spirit of God lives in you. That is real power! If the Holy Spirit of God could raise a dead man to new life, He can certainly give you all you need to break free from your addictions. Renew your mind with that truth. Walk in that truth. When you feel weak and discouraged, stand upon that truth. When the enemy begins to fill your mind with doubts, remember this divine power you possess within.

In light of this great truth, how should we then live? I return to the Apostle Paul's words in Romans 6:1-2: *"What shall we say then? Shall we continue in sin that grace may abound?"* Paul has been discussing the truth that we are saved by grace through faith. In the previous chapter, Romans 5:2, Paul said: *"into this grace in which we stand."* He goes on in Romans 6:15 to discuss *"the free gift"* and *"the gift by the grace of the one Man, Jesus Christ."* It is within this context that Paul's asks the question, *"Since it is all about God's grace then we can just live in sin, right?"* Paul's answer to that is recorded in the next verse: *"Certainly not! How shall we who died to sin live any longer in it?"* (Romans 6:2). In verse 4, Paul writes that we should *"walk in newness of life."*

I sometimes hear people, who really do not understand God's wonderful life-changing grace, ask the question, "Do you mean that since we are saved by grace, we can live any way we want to live?" My answer to that is "absolutely yes!" Now, before you stop reading my book and say, "I do not agree with Pastor Mike!" hear me out. As a Christian, I am able to live as I want. The key is to remember that I no longer want the same things I used to want. I do not want to go to the same places I used to go. I do not want to engage in the activities I once engaged in. I do not want to return to the life I lived before I met Christ. God has given to me a brand new "wanter." So yes, I can live as I want now that I have been born again. But now, I no longer want the things I used to want.

That means there is going to be a clear and evident change seen in my life by others as well. Just as an apple tree bears apples, our lives should show forth fruits which reflect our profession that we are saved. Jesus spoke of this in Matthew 7:17-20: *"Even so, every good tree bears good fruit, but a bad tree bears bad fruit. A good tree cannot bear bad fruit, nor can a bad tree bear good fruit. Every tree that does not bear good fruit is cut down and thrown into the fire. Therefore by their fruits you will know them."* What are the fruits a Christian should bear? In Galatians 5:22-23 they are referred to as "the fruit of the Spirit." *"But the fruit of the Spirit is love, joy, peace, longsuffering, kindness, goodness, faithfulness, gentleness, self-control. Against such there is no law"* (Galatians 5:22-23). These are the evidences of a person who has been born-again because these are present within the new man in the Person and power of the Holy Spirit.

Is it always easy for me as a born-again Christian to continually bear the fruit of the Spirit? No! Sometimes it is very difficult, but it is nonetheless always possible. I still have the influence left behind by the old man who was crucified. I must choose on a daily basis to allow the Holy Spirit to control me, instead of being under the influence of the old person I was before I came to Christ.

The Apostle Paul knew this struggle all too well: *"For what I am doing, I do not understand. For what I will to do, that I do not practice; but what I hate, that I do. If, then, I do what I will not to do, I agree with the law that it is good. But now, it is no longer I who do it, but sin that dwells in me. For I know that in me (that is, in my flesh) nothing good dwells; for to will is present with me, but how to perform what is good I do not find. For the good that I will to do, I do not do; but the evil I will not to do, that I practice. Now if I do what I will not to do, it is no longer I who do it, but sin that dwells in me. I find then a law, that evil is present with me, the one who wills to do good. For I delight in the law of God according to the inward man. But I see another law in my members, warring against the law of my mind, and bringing me into captivity to the law of sin which is in my members. O wretched man that I am! Who will deliver me from this body of death?"* (Romans 7:15-24).

What in the world is wrong with Paul? What is he talking about? Paul is referring to the battle within every born again believer. We have the Spirit of God within, but we also have the influence of the old person remaining. These two are polar opposites. Paul says that he finds it difficult at times to do the things that he knows he should be doing and so easy at times to do the wrong.

Did you notice Paul's conclusion? *"O wretched man that I am!"* Paul understood that he is not everything he should be. I am thankful that God is still working on me. Like Paul, I am not always everything I should be but I am so much more of what God desires me to be today than I have ever been before. Paul gives us the answer to this dilemma. Indeed, our answer is found in his answer to his own question. Paul asked in verse 24: *"Who will deliver me from this body of death?"* The answer is found in the very next verse: *"I thank God-through Jesus Christ our Lord!"* My hope is found in Him. Jesus offers me the power to change and live my life for Him.

It is not always easy, and at times I fail, but I am striving to live my life to glorify my Lord. As I live with that goal, the fruit produced in my life will be consistent with my new birth.

There is a promise that God offers to us that can help you in this struggle to overcome temptation. This promise has helped me many times to overcome the tempter. It is recorded in 1 Corinthians 10:13: *"No temptation has overtaken you except such as is common to man; but God is faithful, who will not allow you to be tempted beyond what you are able, but with the temptation will also make the way of escape, that you may be able to bear it."* That is a promise from God who always keeps His Word. *"God is not a man, that He should lie"* (Numbers 23:19). You can count on what God says every single time. It is against God's very nature to *not* be true to His promises.

There is a promise recorded in 1 Corinthians 10:13 that offers us great strength and assurance. First of all, it reminds us that when we are tempted we are not the only one facing this temptation. *"No temptation has overtaken you except such as is common to man...."* Do not allow the enemy to convince you that you are the only one being attacked with this temptation. Do not begin to think that something is wrong with you that is not wrong with others. We all have the same problem and this problem is nothing new. King Solomon declared in Ecclesiastes 1:9: *"There is nothing new under the sun."* Find comfort in knowing that others have struggled with these temptations before you. Our enemy may have different tools to use in his attack, such as the Internet today, but the temptations are the same. The struggles you face are not unique to you alone. Others have, and do, and will struggle in the same manner.

Also, find great strength in knowing that Jesus too was tempted just as you are, yet He overcame. The writer of Hebrews declares: *"For we do not have a High Priest who cannot sympathize with our weaknesses, but was in all* points *tempted as* we are, yet *without sin"* (Hebrews 4:15). Our Lord knows your struggles and walks with you through each one of them.

The promise of 1 Corinthians 10:13 also assures us that God is *always* faithful. He will never allow the temptation to be so great in our lives that we cannot overcome it. God will either give you the strength you need to bear it, or He will open a way of escape. Sometimes the best thing to do is to run. I think of young Joseph and how his brothers sold him into slavery thinking they were getting rid of him. God however had other plans. It was by God's providence that Joseph became a leader in Egypt. Joseph endured many trials before God raised him up as a great leader in Egypt. One such trial is recorded in Genesis 39:

> *¹ Now Joseph had been taken down to Egypt. And Potiphar, an officer of Pharaoh, captain of the guard, an Egyptian, bought him from the Ishmaelites who had taken him down there.*
> *² The Lord was with Joseph, and he was a successful man; and he was in the house of his master the Egyptian.*

³ And his master saw that the Lord was with him and that the Lord made all he did to prosper in his hand.

⁴ So Joseph found favor in his sight, and served him. Then he made him overseer of his house, and all that he had he put under his authority.

⁵ So it was, from the time that he had made him overseer of his house and all that he had, that the Lord blessed the Egyptian's house for Joseph's sake; and the blessing of the Lord was on all that he had in the house and in the field.

⁶ Thus he left all that he had in Joseph's hand, and he did not know what he had except for the bread which he ate. Now Joseph was handsome in form and appearance.

⁷ And it came to pass after these things that his master's wife cast longing eyes on Joseph, and she said, "Lie with me."

⁸ But he refused and said to his master's wife, "Look, my master does not know what is with me in the house, and he has committed all that he has to my hand.

⁹ There is no one greater in this house than I, nor has he kept back anything from me but you, because you are his wife. How then can I do this great wickedness, and sin against God?"

¹⁰ So it was, as she spoke to Joseph day by day, that he did not heed her, to lie with her or to be with her.

¹¹ But it happened about this time, when Joseph went into the house to do his work, and none of the men of the house was inside,

¹² that she caught him by his garment, saying, "Lie with me." But he left his garment in her hand, and fled and ran outside.

¹³ And so it was, when she saw that he had left his garment in her hand and fled outside,

14 that she called to the men of her house and spoke to them, saying, "See, he has brought in to us a Hebrew to mock us. He came in to me to lie with me, and I cried out with a loud voice.

15 And it happened, when he heard that I lifted my voice and cried out, that he left his garment with me, and fled and went outside."

16 So she kept his garment with her until his master came home.

17 Then she spoke to him with words like these, saying, "The Hebrew servant whom you brought to us came in to me to mock me;

18 so it happened, as I lifted my voice and cried out, that he left his garment with me and fled outside."

19 So it was, when his master heard the words which his wife spoke to him, saying, "Your servant did to me after this manner," that his anger was aroused.

20 Then Joseph's master took him and put him into the prison, a place where the king's prisoners were confined. And he was there in the prison.

21 But the Lord was with Joseph and showed him mercy, and He gave him favor in the sight of the keeper of the prison.

22 And the keeper of the prison committed to Joseph's hand all the prisoners who were in the prison; whatever they did there, it was his doing.

23 The keeper of the prison did not look into anything that was under Joseph's authority, because the Lord was with him; and whatever he did, the Lord made it prosper.

What an interesting account we find recorded here. Joseph had been placed under the authority of Potiphar who was the highest guard under the King of Egypt. And Joseph found himself facing temptation. Potiphar's wife attempted to seduce young Joseph one day while her husband was away. The Bible tells us that Joseph left her presence as quickly as he could. He ran and escaped this temptation, leaving his coat in the seductress' hands. God made a way of escape for Joseph to be the godly man he was called to be. Even in the end—after Joseph was falsely accused, condemned, and imprisoned—God faithfully provided for him and blessed him.

There are a few things I want you to notice in this encounter that Joseph experienced with Potiphar's wife. First of all understand who it is the devil targets. It is one of God's people that he so fiercely wages war against.

The reason the devil could not defeat Joseph is the same reason that he cannot defeat you unless you allow him to do so. This reason is revealed to us in verse 2: *"For God was with him..."* My friend, you can walk in newness of life when you remember that you do not walk alone. You can actually count it a compliment if you are tempted because that simply means you must be a threat to the enemy. This temptation did not come against Joseph because he was guilty of wrong-doing. This temptation came upon him because he was doing exactly what God wanted him to do. His life was bearing fruit for Christ. He had become a threat to the devil. Does your life present any threat to our enemy? Does the devil laugh at you, or does he tremble?

I also want you to see how the enemy enters into our situations, attempting to lure us away. All this began for Joseph with a simple suggestion. Do you see that? It is recorded in verse 7 as Potiphar's wife gave Joseph her invitation: *"Lie with me. Come to bed with me."* She was very suggestive in her indecent proposal.

The enemy comes against us in the same manner. First of all, there is a simple suggestion. Joseph could have made excuses and given into the temptation. Have you ever thought about that? Joseph could have reasoned within himself and rationalized this whole encounter by saying, "Well, I have served the Lord all these years and look where it has gotten me." That is not what Joseph did. He would not give into the temptation. Why did Joseph stand so firmly on his convictions? He knew that it was wrong to do what this woman was asking him to do. There is a good reason to do right because it is the right thing to do! It is as simple as that.

There is much we can learn about overcoming temptation from the young man named Joseph. Notice how Joseph resisted this temptation. He left his garment and ran, probably as fast as he could run. There is a time to stand, but there is also a time to flee. Make up your mind now, *before* the temptation ever comes your way. Decide right now that you are going to resist it no matter what. Go ahead and make up your mind that you are not going to return to your old way of life. The addictions are over. Make the choice *now* to move ahead in your new walk with God.

I heard a story many years ago about an older gentleman who had loved sports all his life. He loved to attend ballgames and cheer his favorite teams on to victory. In high school and college he actually played on the football team. This man was involved in a terrible farming accident one day in which he lost his right arm at the elbow. Depression and despondency begin to settle into his heart. He felt as though life would never be enjoyable again. He became so discouraged that he even stopped attending ballgames. He was devastated. One day a friend convinced him to go out and play some handball with him for exercise. This man with one arm discovered that he was pretty good at this sport. He began playing handball on a regular basis and before long he became very competitive at playing this sport. He even began to play in tournaments and won many of those, even over men much younger than he. People were amazed at how well this one-armed man could play handball. People were fascinated by his story and determination. Well, the newspaper came to interview this man and the reporter asked him, "How did you do it?" The man responded, "Decisions." The reporter, of course, was not satisfied with that simple response so she asked him, "What do you mean by "decisions?" He answered, "Well, it's simple. When the ball comes at my opponent, he has to immediately decide if he is going to hit that ball with his right hand or his left hand? When the ball is swirling toward me, I have already decided." That is what we must do. Decide right now to overcome and even flee if need be.

God will give you all you need to be the godly person He desires you to be. God did it for Joseph and God will do it for you. Claim that promise of 1 Corinthians 10:13.

Living out the Christian life is not about turning over a new leaf. It is not about trying harder or self-reformation. It is not like making a New Year's resolution that you are going to be a better person. This living out the resurrection life is not even about religion or religious ordinances.

I remember when I was twelve years old, walking the aisle of East Tenth Street Church of Christ in Washington, North Carolina. I remember going forward in that service because my friend Andy had recently taken the same step. I do not remember what happened next, but I know I was baptized and added to the membership of that local congregation. I really thought that walking the aisle in a church service and being baptized made me a Christian. I had head knowledge, but inside I remained unchanged. I had gained a little religion, but my heart was untouched and my soul was just as lost as it ever was. I soon became disappointed with my so-called salvation experience. Nothing had really changed within me. I ended up drifting out of the church.

My life began to take a downward turn into the world of drugs and alcohol. It was not until later in life that the Holy Spirit revealed to me from God's Word that what I needed was not some religious ordinance. What I needed was Jesus and His resurrection life in me. Once I surrendered to Him and determined in my heart to live for Him, I was able to walk away from my past and into a future so bright and so hopeful that words fail me in attempting to describe its beauty.

Temptations still taunt me. However, I know in Christ I have all I need to resist and to be the man God has called me to be. I choose to worship only Him. My life has been clean from alcohol and drug abuse now for over twenty-five years, but I know I must remain diligent against temptation.

For a period of about twelve months following my salvation decision at the age of twenty-seven, there were some very strong temptations trying to pull me back into the life from which I had been delivered. It was during those moments of intense temptation that I simply stood on the promise of 1 Corinthians 10:13 and drew as close to God as I could through prayer, Bible study, and active participation in a Bible-believing church. At the end of that twelve-month period of time, I realized that I was now walking in freedom from my past, in a new resurrection life that God had granted me through His grace.

I came to the place where I began to realize that the pull of old addictions was fading into the vast shadows of yesterday. I began to realize the power of His resurrection life within me. Today I am no longer an alcoholic. Today I am no longer a drug addict. Today I have been delivered and healed. I have been empowered by God's presence in my life. This resurrection life can be yours today.

PRAYER: *"I know, Dear God, that I am now a new creation. You have not simply remodeled my old nature, but You have granted unto me a brand new nature. I have Your resurrection life in me. When the enemy comes against me to steal, kill, and destroy, I can be victorious over his schemes because of You. You have granted me all I need to live a victorious Christian life. That is my desire. I never want to return to the life from which You have delivered me. Your life is now my life. In Jesus' name, Amen."*

ASSIGNMENT 7

ARISE TO WALK IN NEWNESS OF LIFE

1. Memorize 1 Corinthians 10:13. Once you have it memorized write it out below:

   _____

   _____

2. Write in your own words what 1 Corinthians 10:13 means to you.

   _____

   _____

3. A city without a wall is wide open for the enemy to overtake it. Read Proverbs 25:28. What are some very practical things that you can do that will act as bricks in the wall to protect you from temptation? (For example, changing the places you go or the people you associate with). List these on the wall which appears below:

TEMPTATION

Proverbs 25:28

87

4. Read Ephesians 4:22-24. This passage is a "change passage." It speaks of "putting off" and "putting on." List below in the appropriate columns what you need to "put off" and then what it is you should "put on" in its place.

PUT OFF: PUT ON:

_____   _____
_____   _____
_____   _____
_____   _____
_____   _____
_____   _____
_____   _____

5. You need to restructure your life! Think of the times when you are tempted the greatest (a certain time of the day or night? In certain situations? On payday? When you are discouraged? Etc.). Identify those times below:

_____
_____
_____

6. How can you restructure your life to protect you from those situations which you identified above? For example, places you used to frequent or people you used to fellowship with. Think about your answers to question 3.

_____
_____
_____

7. Return to those you have wronged in the past. If you have stolen from others, attempt to make it right by returning or repaying what you have stolen. Do as Zacchaeus did following his life-changing encounter with Jesus: Luke 19:8:*"Then Zacchaeus stood and said to the Lord, 'Look, Lord, I give half of my goods to the poor; and if I have taken anything from anyone by false accusation, I restore fourfold."*

8. The Bible says: *"If he gives back what he took in pledge for a loan, returns what he has stolen, follows the decrees that give life, and does no evil, he will surely live; he will not die. None of the sins he has committed will be remembered against him. He has done what is just and right; he will surely live"* (Ezekiel 33:15-16).

LIVING AS A VICTOR—NOT A VICTIM

"Therefore do not let sin reign in your mortal body, that you should obey it in its lusts. And do not present your members as instruments of unrighteousness to sin, but present yourselves to God as being alive from the dead, and your members as instruments of righteousness to God. For sin shall not have dominion over you, for you are not under law but under grace."
Romans 6:12-14

You do not have to live under your circumstances any longer. You can rise above the problems and struggles of your past. You no longer have to live your life as a victim. You can now live a life that is victorious over those things which have held you captive in your past. This is not always easy, but it is always possible for those who have placed their faith in Jesus as their Lord and Savior. You are now a Spirit-empowered child of the King! You now have royal blood flowing through your veins. Live out who you are in Christ Jesus.

First of all, listen to what God says about you. This message of truth from your Creator may be in direct contrast with what others are saying about you or maybe even with what you have been saying about yourself. I ask you, "Whose evaluation of your identity is more trustworthy? Is it God's, others, or your own?" I think you get my point. We can always trust God's Word to be perfectly trustworthy and reliable. His Word is indeed the *truth* that is able to set us free.

What does God say about who you are now? Please open your heart and listen to God speak to you through Ephesians 1:

God tells me that I am chosen by Him! Ephesians 1:4: *"... just as He chose us in Him before the foundation of the world, that we should be holy and without blame before Him in love... ."*

To ponder this eternal truth that I am chosen by God fills my heart with humility and amazement. Looking back on my childhood, I remember myself as a rather awkward adolescent, struggling with acne and a poor evaluation of myself. I always wanted to fit in with those who were the most popular, but always felt that I never could.

In junior high school I was always one of the last ones chosen during physical education when the captains chose their teams. Sometimes I felt as if the two team captains were going to actually fight over which team was going to be burdened with me. Now I know that I am chosen by God Himself. Wow! The Creator of all the world, chose me! The One who one day so long ago gazed down into nothingness and purposed in Himself to form earth and to place the stars into the Milky Way, chose me. The One who is omniscient, omnipotent, and omnipresent chose me! I am of great eternal value.

God tells me that I am adopted as His son! Ephesians 1-5: *"having predestined us to adoption as sons by Jesus Christ to Himself, according to the good pleasure of His will... ."*

It was part of God's plan from the very beginning to save me and to bring me unto Himself. This concept of adoption spoken of here does not refer to our salvation as much as it does to the benefits of our salvation. We are saved by being born into God's family. This new birth, or regeneration, begins the moment a person believes in Christ as his or her personal Lord and Savior. Now, we were all born into this world as babies—correct? People do not enter into this world as toddlers, or as teenagers, or as adults. Just as we are born as infants physically, we are also born as "babes in Christ" spiritually, the moment Christ saves us. Paul wrote to the people in Corinth addressing their many problems in *1 Corinthians 3:1*: *"And I, brethren, could not speak to you as to spiritual people but as to carnal, as to babes in Christ."*

According to ancient Roman law, and it is basically still true today, a baby could not claim his or her inheritance until he or she became of adult age. So, what has God done for me? He has brought me into His family through regeneration and justification. This is the act whereby I am born again. However, at the same time, God also adopts me as an adult spiritual son who can immediately begin accessing his inheritance and benefits as His child. Immediately upon salvation, God extends to me love, joy, peace, longsuffering, kindness, goodness, faithfulness, gentleness, and the power to exercise self-control (Galatians 5:22-23). Who am I? I am a born-again, adopted, blood-bought, redeemed, empowered, eternally rich and currently blessed child of God. That's not self-esteem but that is God esteem!

God tells me that I am accepted! Ephesians 1:6: *"to the praise of the glory of His grace, by which He has made us accepted in the Beloved."*

I am not accepted because I am good enough, but I am accepted because of God's grace. When God looks upon my soul, He no longer sees the ugliness of my sin. God now sees Jesus and His imputed righteousness. I am covered from head to toe with Jesus. Now as God looks upon me, He no longer sees my unrighteousness, but He sees only Christ's righteousness which makes me acceptable to Him.

God tells me that I am redeemed and forgiven! Ephesians 1:7: *"… In Him we have redemption through His blood, the forgiveness of sins, according to the riches of His grace."*

The word *redemption* means "to ransom in full."[6] My sin debt

---

[6] James Strong, S.T.D., LL.D., *The Exhaustive Concordance of The Bible* (Peabody, MA: Hendrickson Publishers), #629, p.14.

has been paid in full. In Paul's day, this word was used to describe someone purchasing a slave and then simply releasing that slave to be free.[7] My debt has been paid in full and I am now forgiven. I choose to no longer listen to the lies from the enemy telling me that I am guilty, unworthy, unloved, and unforgiven. I know it is only through Jesus' blood and by His grace but I am redeemed and forgiven.

God tells me that I have been sealed! Ephesians 1:13: *"In Him you also trusted, after you heard the word of truth, the gospel of your salvation; in whom also, having believed, you were sealed with the Holy Spirit of promise... ."*

This truth brings certainty to my salvation experience. I am secure in Christ and in God's family. This is a finished transaction.[8] In ancient days there were several uses for a seal:

1. A seal would confirm something as being genuine.
2. A seal would identify personal property.
3. A seal was used to make something secure.[9]

All three of these uses can be applied to my life as a born-again, adopted, child of God. First of all, this seal makes me a genuine Christian. God is the One who does the sealing.

Secondly, I now belong to God and Him alone. This means that I am not to worship other gods. I am not to allow anyone or anything else to control me. I belong exclusively to Him. I am His property.

Thirdly, this seal guarantees my full salvation. I am secure in Christ and nothing or no one can ever change that. Ephesians 4:30 reminds us that we are sealed *"for the day of redemption."* That will

---

[7] Warren W. Wiersbe, *The Bible Expositional Commentary (BE Series),* New Testament, Volume 2, (Database @ 2007 WORDsearch Corp.), p.11.

[8] Ibid., p.12.

[9] Charles Hodge, *A Commentary on Ephesians,* (database@2004 WORDsearch Corp., Ephesians 1:13.

be the day of full redemption when I stand justified, sanctified, and glorified in the presence of God. In the meantime, I can trust God to transform my life into His image. He is going to finish what He has begun in me. Philippians 1:6: *"being confident of this very thing, that He who has begun a good work in you will complete it until the day of Jesus Christ."*

The truth of God sets me free to be who I am in Christ. I no longer live as a victim, enslaved by my past mistakes and controlled by my natural man, but I now walk in victory. This victory was not realized in my life through some man-made twelve-step program. I actually took only one step. That one step was the step I took in 1988 when I surrendered to the Holy Spirit's prompting and invited Jesus to be my Lord and my Savior. That was the day of my deliverance and salvation. That was also the beginning of a brand new life. Each day I live, I must choose to be victorious over my past and over the temptation that comes upon me.

It is a daily choice I make to live as a victor and not a victim. What choice have you made? Will you choose to live the same empty and destructive lifestyle that you have lived in your past? Or will you choose life today? Stop living as a victim and start living in the victory Christ offers.

This struggle to live in victory takes place in my thinking. I must think about myself as God now sees me, so I can live righteously before God. What does that mean? The Bible teaches in Proverbs 23:7: *"For as he thinks in his heart, so is he... ."* If you listen to the lies of Satan, you will always struggle. Your thoughts concerning yourself will be extremely negative and degrading. The result will be a life lived in defeat. Do not be a victim. Remember who you are, my friend. You have been chosen, adopted, accepted, redeemed, forgiven, and sealed. You are saved and secure in God's family. The truth concerning all born-again, adopted believers is that we are children of the King who immediately have access to everything we need from our Father Who is in heaven.

PRAYER: *"Dear wonderful Heavenly Father, Giver of every good and perfect gift, my heart worships You. You and You alone have given me the victory over sin. Sin no longer has a hold on my life. I accept the truth of who You say that I am. Help me to put off the lies that I have believed for so long. I desire to renew my mind with Your truth. Help me to understand the truth about the world around me, and who I am through Your eyes. It is Your truth that sets me free. I desire to always live in Your freedom. Thank You, my God. In Jesus' name, Amen."*

ASSIGNMENT 8

LIVING AS A VICTOR—NOT A VICTIM

1. Memorize James 4:7. Write it out here:

   _____

   _____

   _____

   _____

2. Read Philippians 4:8. What do you think? This verse tells us how we should be thinking. Write the key words given in this verse concerning the type of things you are to be thinking. *Whatsoever things are:*

   _____

   _____

   _____

   _____

   _____

3. How can I apply Philippians 4:8 to my thoughts concerning who I am in Christ and living out the victorious Christian life?

   _____

   _____

   _____

   _____

   _____

4. Read Ephesians 6:10-18. List the different parts of the Armor of God:

a.

b.

c.

d.

e.

f.

5. 1 Corinthians 15:57: *"But thanks be to God, who gives us the victory through our Lord Jesus Christ."* What is it that you need victory over?

_____

_____

_____

6. Who do you say that you are? Place a check beside each statement below that you believe is true about you. Then read the corresponding scripture beside that statement and write below it what God says about you.

_____ I cannot break the power of sin. (Romans 6:6, 11, 17- 18)

_____ Nobody really loves me. (Ephesians 2:4, 5:1-2, John 15:9)

_____ I don't have enough faith. (Romans 10:17; Hebrews 12:2)

_____ I don't have what it takes to live right. (Philippians 4:19)

_____ I am hopeless. (Hebrews 6:19; Romans 15:13)

_____ I am a failure. (2 Corinthians 3:5-6)

_____ I am going crazy. (1 Corinthians 2:16)

_____ I am afraid. (1 John 4:18; 2 Timothy 1:7)

_____ I'm not strong enough. (Romans 8:9-11; Ephesians 1:19)

_____ I'm condemned. (Romans 8:1; Colossians 1:22)

_____ I am guilty. (Hebrews 10:10; Colossians 1:14)

SUPPORTING ONE ANOTHER

"But exhort one another daily, while it is called 'Today,'
lest any of you be hardened through the deceitfulness of sin."
Hebrews 3:13

God has not created us to be independent creatures in need of nothing, but we are created as very dependent beings. In fact, we are very needy. We need food, water, shelter, and companionship. We need oxygen to breathe. We need a controlled climate, not too hot and not too cold. *We need God.* There is only One Sovereign Being in the universe and that is God Almighty. Psalm 103:19 declares: *"The LORD has established His throne in heaven, And His kingdom rules over all."* We are creatures totally dependent upon the Creator.

We also need one another. In the creation account recorded in Genesis, we learn that God created everything within a six-day period of time, resting on the seventh day. At the end of the first five days of creation, God spoke a benediction in relation to what He had created. A benediction is a blessing. That benediction or blessing God spoke was *"and it was good."* The Bible records God making that statement at the end of each of the first five days of creation (Genesis 1:4, 10, 12, 18, 21 and 25).

However, at the end of the sixth day, God spoke a malediction. A malediction is not a blessing, but a curse. God created man during that sixth day of creation. He then looked upon man and declared: *"It is not good."* (Genesis 2:18). What is not good? That man is alone. What was God's answer to this problem? God created Eve, a companion who was created especially for Adam. We all need companionship. We all need support from one another.

The gift of salvation is a gift that God gives to the believing sinner. Justification is a sovereign act of God. We receive that act of justification from God by grace through faith. The work of sanctification, however, requires our ongoing and active participation. Sanctification, unlike justification, is a process and not an act. Sanctification is a lifetime process in which the believer is learning and growing in the faith. In this life, we are ever becoming and never fully arriving.

The Christian life is referred to in the Bible as a *walk* and not a *rest*. Sanctification requires not only our own personal participation, but many times the participation of others in our lives to aid us in this growth process. Paul writes in Romans 10:14-17: *"How then shall they call on Him in Whom they have not believed? And how shall they believe in Him of Whom they have not heard? And how shall they hear without a preacher? And how shall they preach unless they are sent? As it is written: 'How beautiful are the feet of those who preach the gospel of peace, who bring glad tidings of good things!' But they have not all obeyed the gospel. For Isaiah says, 'Lord, who has believed our report?' So then faith comes by hearing, and hearing by the word of God."* We need others in our lives who are sent to proclaim God's truth that we might believe. How will we hear unless someone tells us the truth of the gospel?

The local church should serve a vital purpose in the life of every believer. Each member of the local church is important and intrinsically interconnected with the other members. You are important to the body of Christ. There is a special place within the body where God desires you to serve alongside other believers. You have been saved and equipped to minister in a specific area of service. As each member within the church serves by exercising his or her spiritual gifts, the church is enabled to be the living and world-changing organism that God desires. There is a place for you in the church! Your fellow believers need you, just as you need them.

The parallel comparison that scripture gives us of this truth is the example of the human body. Every member of your body is connected and dependent upon the other members. What good is a hand without an arm? How about a foot without a leg? A body without a heart? Paul wrote about this in 1 Corinthians 12:13-27: *"For as the body is one and has many members, but all the members of that one body, being many, are one body, so also is Christ. For by one Spirit we were all baptized into one body--whether Jews or Greeks, whether slaves or free--and have all been made to drink into one Spirit. For in fact the body is not one member but many. If the foot should say, 'Because I am not a hand, I am not of the body,' is it therefore not of the body? And if the ear should say, 'Because I am not an eye, I am not of the body,' is it therefore not of the body? If the whole body were an eye, where would be the hearing? If the whole were hearing, where would be the smelling? But now God has set the members, each one of them, in the body just as He pleased. And if they were all one member, where would the body be? But now indeed there are many members, yet one body. And the eye cannot say to the hand, 'I have no need of you'; nor again the head to the feet, 'I have no need of you.' No, much rather, those members of the body which seem to be weaker are necessary. And those members of the body which we think to be less honorable, on these we bestow greater honor; and our unpresentable parts have greater modesty, but our presentable parts have no need. But God composed the body, having given greater honor to that part which lacks it, that there should be no schism in the body, but that the members should have the same care for one another. And if one member suffers, all the members suffer with it; or if one member is honored, all the members rejoice with it. Now you are the body of Christ, and members individually."*

The context in which Paul penned those words was one of great division within the church at Corinth. They were divided into small cliques and special interest groups. They were even refusing to fellowship with one another during a common meal! Paul addressed these believers and reminded them how they needed one another.

Many times we find the Bible referring to our interconnectedness with the phrase *one another*. Read with me, a few of those[10]:

- John 13:14: *"Wash one another's feet."*
- Romans 12:10: *"Be kindly affectionate to one another..."*
- Romans 12:10: *"Giving preference to one another."*
- Romans 12:16: *"Be of the same mind one toward another."*
- Romans 14:13: *"Do not judge one another."*
- James 4:11: *"Do not speak evil one of another."*
- Romans 14:19: *"Edify one another."*
- Romans 15:7: *"Receive one another."*
- Romans 15:14: *"Admonish one another."*
- 1 Corinthians 12:25: *"Care for one another."*
- 1 Peter 4:10: *"Minister gifts one to another."*
- 1 Corinthians 16:20: *"Greet one another."*
- Galatians 5:13: *"Serve one another."*
- Galatians 6:2: *"Bear one another's burdens."*
- Ephesians 5:21: *"Submit one to another."*
- 1 Thessalonians 4:18: *"Comfort one another."*
- Hebrews 3:13: *"Exhort one another."*
- Hebrews 10:24: *"Consider one another."*
- James 5:16: *"Confess your faults one to another."*
- James 5:16: *"Pray one for another."*
- 1 Peter 4:9: *"Use hospitality one to another."*
- 1 John 1:7: *"Fellowship with one another."*

My friend, when you made the decision to follow Christ, that was your final independent decision. From that point onward, every

---

[10] Adrain Rogers, *The Adrian Rogers Legacy Collection*, The Church-The Body of Christ, New testament, 1 Corinthians 12. © 2011 Rogers Family Trust. (Database © 2011 WORDsearch Corp).

decision you face should be approached by asking God, "What do You want me to do?"

First of all, get involved in a local church serving our Lord with fellow believers as you exercise your spiritual gifts. The local church is here for your benefit. The writer of Hebrews 10:25 exhorts us: *"not forsaking the assembling of ourselves together, as is the manner of some, but exhorting* one another, *and so much the more as you see the Day approaching."* We need to assemble together as the church to exhort, which means to comfort, entreat, and to invite to come near. The majority of the time that the word *church* appears in the Bible, it refers to a local church. God has placed the church among us to help us.

Secondly, have a time set aside each day to study God's Word and pray. You need to grow in your faith. Growth cannot take place apart from nourishment. Donald Whitney, in his book *Spiritual Disciplines for the Christian Life* writes: "There is simply no healthy Christian life apart from a diet of the milk and meat of Scripture."[11] There are many Bible studies available, just like this one, to aid you in your deliverance from addiction. Many helpful resources can be found on the Internet. The website settingcaptivesfree.com offers donation-based online programs that help with overcoming addictions and many other problems that people face in life. Get involved in a regular Bible study program.

Thirdly, surround yourself with godly people. If you are constantly associating with your old friends who are living lives of idolatry, you will struggle to live out this new life of freedom. The Psalmist declared in Psalm 119:115: *"Depart from me, you evildoers, For I will keep the commandments of my God!"* The writer of Proverbs tells us in Proverbs 4:14-15: *"Do not enter the path of the wicked, And do not walk in the way of evil. Avoid it, do not travel on it; Turn away from it and pass on."* There is an ancient Oriental proverb that says, "If you

---

[11] Donald S. Whitney, *Spiritual Disciplines For the Christian Life*, (Colorado Springs, Colorado; 19910, p.24.

lie down with dogs you will rise up with fleas." Be careful about the company you keep.

Be careful that you choose friends that are striving to walk in holiness as you are. Amos 3:3 *"Can two walk together, unless they are agreed?"* Those with whom you associate should be in agreement with you concerning how we should live our lives. Those around you can either build you up or they can tear you down. Proverbs 27:17 teaches: *"As iron sharpens iron, So a man sharpens the countenance of his friend."*

Lastly, allow others to hold you accountable. This requires that you confide in a few close friends whom you know you can trust. Be real. Be honest about your struggles and the wonderful work that God is doing in your life. James 5:16: *"Confess your trespasses to one another, and pray for one another, that you may be healed."* Ask these close friends, or family members, to pray for you. Also invite them to ask you on a regular basis how you are doing. These need to be loved ones who sincerely care about you and want to see you succeed in living out your new victorious life for Christ.

PRAYER: *"Dear God in Heaven, I confess that I am not an independent and self-sufficient creature. I need You every minute of every day and every night. You have all that I need. I need you. I also need to be a faithful part of Your body as represented in the local church. Please guide my path to that community of believers with whom You want me to serve. Lord, I need the support of others and I desire to offer that same support to those around me. My desire is to be a healthy and active member of Your body. Show me where You would have me to serve and what You would have me to be. I am asking, seeking, and knocking. In Jesus' name, Amen."*

ASSIGNMENT 9

CHAPTER NINE

SUPPORTING ONE ANOTHER

1. Attend a Bible-believing and Bible-preaching church at least once each week.

2. Spend a daily time in prayer when you ask God to help you walk in victory.

3. Ask a Christian friend of the same sex to help hold you accountable. If you do not know who to ask, pray about this and ask God to give you discernment. This person should be trustworthy and willing to check on you regularly.

4. As a member of the body, you should function in a manner which helps the other members. Look for ways that you can minister to others this week. Every member is important and should be serving faithfully in ministry.

Group Study Guidelines

To help you implement the chapters of this book into a group setting, the following study guides for each chapter have been included. This group study can be conducted in a nine-week period of time. However, be flexible. The study may be lengthened depending on how much discussion is generated during your meeting. Discussion should be encouraged even if the study needs to be extended past the suggested nine-week period of time. Try to get everyone actively involved. People retain only 10% of what they hear. They retain 90% of what they hear, see, and do.

Encourage those participating to bring their Bibles, a notepad, and a pen to each session. Note taking is a good idea.

Adult schedules are usually very demanding and extra encouragement for participants from the leader of the group will be beneficial during the week. Between sessions, try to contact each member by email, telephone call, text, or postcard simply to encourage them to press on.

Instruct the participants to read the chapter at least once and complete the assignment for that chapter prior to each group meeting. They may want to write the answers to the assignment questions in their personal notebooks.

EXTRA TIPS FOR GROUP MEETINGS:

1. **Prayer is essential.** Pray for each participant by name each week. Ask God to speak to hearts and change lives. Pray concerning the upcoming meeting that our Lord would be honored in every way. Ask God to lead and guide your group to victorious Christian living.

2. **Begin each meeting with prayer:** Ask if there are any prayer needs among the members about which you can pray. Take time here to really listen to needs and pray about these as a group. Be sensitive to those who may need special prayer. Be willing to take the time to gather around those individuals, laying on hands, and praying out loud.

3. **Make the environment as warm and inviting as possible.** A time of refreshments may be desirable to create an atmosphere of fellowship.

4. **Be certain your meeting environment is one that honors privacy.** Your participants need to know that this is a safe environment where they can share their struggles with fellow believers.

5. **Stay on schedule.** It will only discourage and confuse your group if meetings are continually cancelled and/or rescheduled. Stay within the time frame agreed upon as well, for the duration of the meeting. Start on time. End on time. Respect the time of others.

6. **A smaller group size of ten or less usually works best.** This keeps the meetings more personal and allows time for each to share if desired.

May our Lord fill you with His Spirit as you step forward to be used by Him. Be real with your group. Be honest concerning how you have struggled in the past. Offer the hope that is found only in the Gospel of Jesus our Lord. Continue to bring the group discussions back to what scripture teaches and offer the encouragement found there.

Group Study Guide

Chapter 1

From the Needle to the Bible

Main idea of the chapter: We each have a story to tell of how our lives have been affected by sin. We share a common problem, a sin nature.

Begin with prayer.

Share with the group the main idea of the chapter. Read Romans 3:23: "*for all have sinned and fall short of the glory of God.*" Explain how we all face the same dilemma. We need change in our lives because of the fact that we are all sinners and we all live in a sinful world.

Explain how the Apostle Paul, formerly known as Saul, had the heart of an addict who needed transformation.

Explain how Stephen, a young disciple of the Lord, stood before the religious Jewish council as he was accused of speaking "*blasphemous words*" (Acts 6:13). Ask for a volunteer to read the biblical record of Stephen's stoning in Acts 7:54-60.

Stress that Saul is the man who would become the great missionary, the Apostle Paul.

GROUP STUDY QUESTIONS

1. What was Saul doing while Stephen was being executed? (Acts 7:58).

2. Stephen prayed a prayer just before he died. Read it in Acts 7:60. Does Stephen's prayer remind you of another person's prayer in the Bible?

3. Who is it that we should strive to be like?

Explain how Saul was changed. Although he is seen condoning the murder of Stephen (Acts 7), Saul was later transformed. Ask someone to read Acts 9:1-22.

MORE GROUP DISCUSSION QUESTIONS

4. What or who made a difference in Paul's life?

5. Paul's temporary physical blindness can be a picture of his spiritual blindness before meeting the resurrected Christ. What are some things in your past that you would identify as being a result of your spiritual blindness?

6. The author of *Casting Down Idols* shared in Chapter 1, how his own spiritual blindness led him into a life of drugs and alcohol abuse. Are there elements in the author's story that you can directly relate to? What are those elements?

7. Saul's turning point was on the road to Damascus where he met Christ. Pastor Dixon's turning point was in a mid-week prayer meeting as he knelt at the altar, finally surrendering

to Christ. Ask your group, "Have you had a turning point in your life? Encourage individuals to explain.

8. Allow time for participants to share their personal stories. Be careful here to encourage participants to give God, and not the enemy, all the glory and praise. Share your own testimony if time allows.

Close in prayer.

CHAPTER 2

First Things First

Main idea of the chapter: Salvation needs to take place in a person's heart. We are all sinners in need of a Savior.

Begin with prayer. Ask if anyone has a praise report. Did anyone experience a victory over temptation this week?

Share with the group the main idea of the chapter and explain in your own words.

Review the chapter end assignment questions. Allow those present to share their responses.

GROUP DISCUSSION QUESTIONS

1. What evidence do we have that people are born in sin, with a sinful nature?

2. What have you tried in the past to produce change? What has worked to some degree for you? What attempts have been unsuccessful?

3. Why do you think your past attempts to be free have failed?

4. What was the Apostle Paul's drug of choice? Does it surprise you that religion can be an idol? How do you think this is true?

5. Ask, "What are some of the idols that you see in our world today?" "What idols have been a controlling factor in your life?"

Read together some key passages that were presented in this chapter and allow for discussion:

Romans 3:10-12, 23; 5:1,8; 6:23; 7:15; 8:1, 38-39; 10:9.

Close in prayer.

CHAPTER 3

FACING THE TRUTH: ADMITTING YOUR SIN

Main idea of the chapter: We must see our sin the way that God sees it.

Begin with prayer.

Share with the group the main idea of the chapter and explain in your own words based upon your reading of chapter 3.

Review the chapter end assignment questions. Allow time for those who would like to share their responses.

GROUP DISCUSSION QUESTIONS

1. Have someone read John 8:32. What do you think Jesus meant by *truth*?

2. Some refer to addiction today as *disease*. Experts claim that there is no cure for this so-called disease. What does God call addiction or idolatry?

3. Have someone read Romans 12:3. How does society's model for teaching unconditional self-esteem contrast with what God says? The important thing is not that we help people feel good about themselves. We must help people see themselves as God sees them.

GROUP ACTIVITY

(Allow 5-10 minutes) Instruct your group to break up into groups of 2-3. Together read and discuss Philippians 4:8. Each small group should write out the key words that are given in this verse to evaluate our thoughts.

GROUP DISCUSSION QUESTIONS

4. Share together the lists constructed in the smaller groups. How can we apply this verse to the manner in which we see ourselves? Stress that each one of the descriptive words in Philippian 4:8 are true of God. What is most important is not necessarily what someone has said about us. What is most important is what God says about us now.

5. What are you thinking about? Ask yourself, "Is it true?" What are some lies that you have believed concerning yourself? How do you overcome these false messages?

Close in prayer.

CHAPTER 4

Bull's-Eye Living

Main idea of the chapter: Your main goal in living should be to bring honor and glory to God.

Begin with prayer.

Share with the group the main idea of the chapter and review the chapter end assignment questions. Allow time for sharing.

Ask for a volunteer to read John 4:1-30. This is the account of the Samaritan woman at the well and her life-changing encounter with Jesus.

GROUP DISCUSSION QUESTIONS

1. Can you identify the idol which was sitting on the throne of the Samaritan woman's life? What are some evidences to support your response?

2. What are some other idols that people worship today?

3. Why is it important that we aim for the proper goals in life? (Explain here how we are not saved by works, but by grace. If we are saved, there will be evidence of salvation.)

4. What have been some of your reasons in the past for desiring change?

5. What should be your number reason now?

Ask someone to read 2 Peter 1:2-4.

MORE GROUP DISCUSSION QUESTIONS

6. Identify the two things, according to 2 Peter 1:2-4, that God gives to us so we will have all we need to live victoriously.

7. Complete the statement: "all I want out of life is _____
   _____.

Close in prayer.

CHAPTER 5

A Change of Direction

Main idea of the chapter: Repentance is necessary for change to take place.

Begin with prayer. Allow time for those who are willing, to share how their lives have changed over the past few weeks. How is this study blessing and helping them?

Share with the group the main idea of the chapter and review the chapter end assignment questions. Allow time for sharing.

Note that Pastor Dixon shares how he attempted to run from God's calling on his life for many years. It was when he stopped running from God and turned around toward God, that he discovered this call was a tremendous blessing in his life. Emphasize that God has a plan for each one of them. Encourage them to follow after God's calling in their lives.

Ask for a volunteer to read Psalm 51.

GROUP DISCUSSION QUESTIONS

1. David attempted to cover up the sin he committed with Bathsheba. How have you attempted to conceal your sin?

2. Psalm 51 is a prayer that King David prayed, crying out to God for forgiveness and restoration. What key words can you identify in Psalm 51 that illustrate David's brokenness and true repentance?

GROUP ACTIVITY

(Allow 10 minutes) Instruct the participants to spend a few minutes quietly writing out their own personal prayer of repentance unto God. They can use Psalm 51 as a guide.

MORE GROUP DISCUSSION QUESTIONS

Ask someone to read 1 Corinthians 6:9-11. Psychology classifies addictions under a *disease* model. Psychologists also admit that they have no cure available. Alcoholics Anonymous, for example, teaches that once a person is an alcoholic, he will always be an alcoholic. How does 1 Corinthians 6:9-11 differ from the world's model?

Close with prayer.

CHAPTER 6

ADDICTIONS: DEAD AND BURIED

Main idea of the chapter: As a Christian, the person you used to be is dead.

Begin with prayer. Any praise reports?

Share with the group the main idea of the chapter and review the chapter end assignment questions. Allow time for sharing.

Ask for a volunteer to read Ephesians 2:8. Explain what grace means (undeserved favor).

GROUP DISCUSSION QUESTIONS

1. Since grace is unearned and undeserved, it comes to us without cost. God's grace is, however, very expensive. What did the grace that God extended toward fallen mankind require of Him? (John 3:16).

2. Grace is a *gift* that you receive. Faith is the *act* of your receiving this grace gift of salvation from God. Have you ever received anything that you did not deserve? What are some examples?

3. There were many different responses to the crucifixion of Christ. Some were indifferent. Others were simply filled with unbelief. What does the death of Christ mean to you?

Close in prayer asking God to help each one to keep self on the cross and Jesus on the throne.

CHAPTER 7

ARISE TO WALK IN NEWNESS OF LIFE

Main idea of the chapter: As a Christian, you are now a new person with resurrection life within.

Begin with prayer. Are there any praise reports?

Share with the group the main idea of the chapter and review the chapter end assignment questions. Allow time for sharing.

Ask for a volunteer to read Romans 6:8-11. Allow for open discussion.

GROUP DISCUSSION QUESTIONS

1. According to Romans 6:8-11, Jesus died as us and arose as us. He died and arose in our place! How should that truth impact your everyday life?

2. Jesus promises in John 10:10 that He came to give abundant life. What does that term *abundant life* mean to you?

3. What are some practical ways in which your life is now different?

4. Ask for a volunteer to read Ephesians 4:22-24. This passage is telling us that we must *"put off"* some things and *"put on"* some things. What is right in the middle of this change? Read verse 23 again. We must renew our minds. This is accomplished through God's Word. What are some ways you can get God's Word into your mind?

GROUP ACTIVITY:

(10 minutes) Divide the group into smaller groups with 2-4 people in each sub-group. Give them paper and pencils. Instruct them to draw a line straight down the middle of the page from top to bottom forming two equal columns. Have them label the columns "Put Off" and "Put On." As a group, they are then to brainstorm a list under each column. Challenge them to think biblically. (For example: Put off lying; Put on truth. Why? Because scripture teaches we are to be honest and truthful).

Close in prayer

CHAPTER 8

LIVING AS A VICTOR—NOT A VICTIM

Main idea of the chapter: As a Christian I can now live a victorious Christian life free from addiction.

Begin with prayer. First, receive prayer requests and ask someone to lead in prayer.

Ask a volunteer to read Ephesians 1.

Take time to review the Chapter 8 assignment. Encourage discussion. Ask for a volunteer to recite 1 Corinthians 10:13 from memory. Discuss the importance of that verse.

GROUP DISCUSSION QUESTIONS

1. Living victoriously above our circumstances and over temptation is not always easy. What are some practical changes you can make in your everyday routine which will help you stay strong?

2. What are some important words recorded in Ephesians 1 that identify who you are in Christ?

3. If you believe that you are a failure, then chances are you will fail in your attempts for change. What you believe to be true, whether it is true or not, is going to affect your behavior. How does it help you in overcoming addictions, to understand who you are in Christ?

4. What are some common lies associated with addictions? (For example, "I can quit anytime I want to.") List these on a marker board as the participants respond.

Close in prayer

CHAPTER 9

SUPPORTING ONE ANOTHER

Main idea of the chapter: We are dependent upon God and one another.

Begin with prayer. Ask if anyone has a praise report.

Ask a volunteer to read Hebrews 10:25. Discuss together how we can fulfill this command.

Take time to review the chapter 9 assignment. Encourage discussion.

GROUP DISCUSSION QUESTIONS

1. Brainstorm together things that we all need (food, shelter, water, etc...). It is clear that we are all very needy. We need God and we need one another.

2. Ask for volunteers to share how they first heard the gospel and believed. Stress that they had to hear it from someone else.

3. Proverbs 27:17 teaches: *"As iron sharpens iron, So a man sharpens the countenance of his friend."* How can we sharpen one another?

GROUP ACTIVITY

Divide into smaller groups. Have each group study James 3:1-12. Identify as a group the three types of tongues described. (#1. A bridled tongue, which we all need. #2. A burning tongue. #3. A bitter tongue.)

Discuss together the types of words we can speak that will support others.

Close in prayer.

Scripture Index